It's easy to isolate a verse and make it say something you want it to say. It's more difficult to read it in context and receive that transforming truth. That's the heart of what Jay Payleitner has done in this book.

—Chris Fabry, Award-winning author and host of "Chris Fabry Live" on the Moody Network

Jay Payleitner has always had a wonderful way of teaching profound truths in a way that is fun, instructive, and life changing. Read *The Next Verse* and you will go places and discover truths that will impact how you think about God and His revelations and how you live your life.

—Steve Brown, Professor, broadcaster on "Key Life Network," and best-selling author of *Three Free Sins: God's Not Mad at You* and *Laughter and Lament: The Radical Freedom of Joy and Sorrow*

We've seen some Bible verses so often we stop seeing them. But Jay dares us to trade in bumper sticker theology for something much better: an authentic pondering of God's holy Word. We need this book!

—Jon Gauger, Producer/host on Moody Radio and author of *Kids Say the Wisest Things*

One of Jesus's favorite utterances went like this: "You have heard it said...but I tell you...." That's what Jay Payleitner does in his newest book by examining the context of 60 popular Bible verses. Three pages in you say to yourself, "WOW, that's amazing! I never saw that." Well, that just happened to me 60 times. *The Next Verse* is a rare gem with insight I'll be thinking about for a long time.

—David Murrow, The Online Preaching Coach and author of *Why Men Hate Going to Church*

Ministers, teachers, and authors love to disseminate a wealth of information while often failing miserably at revealing the true context and valuable applications of the Bible verses they tag on to prove their point. In *The Next Verse*, Jay Payleitner shares keen insights that will not only surprise you but encourage you to go deeper into the true meaning and ultimate goal of God's Word—transforming us into the image of Jesus Christ. It's time to stop skimming the surface of Scripture and explore the rich treasures that await, so you may join the psalmist in saying, *"How sweet are your words to my taste, sweeter than honey to my mouth!"* (Psalm 119:103).

—Kay Horner, Executive Director, Awakening America Alliance

I recently read a version of the Bible that had no chapters or verse numbers. It was difficult at first, but I soon learned to appreciate the text even more, unencumbered by divisions. Jay's book is so helpful in the same way. Reading Scripture this way forces us to open up our minds in light of the larger passage!

—Wayne Shepherd, Nationally-known Christian radio host

Jay Payleitner must have been mentored by Bobb Biehl who shares, "Nothing is meaningful without context!" This book instantly drew me in when I realized most of us can quote several favorite Scripture verses, but almost none of us can share from memory the verses immediately preceding or following! Thank you, Jay, for giving all of us the gift of "context" in your fascinating new book *The Next Verse*.

—Bob Tiede, Cru U.S. Leadership Development Team, author of five books including *339 Questions Jesus Asked!*, and blogger at LeadingWithQuestions.com

When I first read the title, I said to myself, *Okay, this isn't anything new.* Then, I read the first chapter, then the next, and finally, the entire book. I was wrong—very wrong! I couldn't wait to read the "next verse" in every chapter. There's a wealth of wisdom for moms, dads, civic leaders, businesspeople and even pastors. *The Next Verse* is packed full of transformative insight while being fun to read. Thanks, Jay! You've listened to the Scriptures and done well.

—Steve Hefta, Strategic Account Manager, Marketplace Chaplains

Jay Payleitner has given us a fascinating take on popular Bible verses. It shows just how talented of a writer he is and a brilliant Bible apologist. This book is an important read whether you are a pastor, lay person, or theologian.

—Rick Johnson, best-selling author of *That's My Son* and *Grandparents Raising Grandchildren*

The Next Verse is a gift to anyone yearning to know more about God. Without preaching at us or making us feel guilty or dumb, Jay Payleitner makes one principle of biblical interpretation easy and fun, and lowers our chances of misinterpreting the Bible.

—Dr. Clarence Shuler, President/CEO, BLR: Building Lasting Relationships

Randomly ripping a verse out of the Bible is like changing lanes on the interstate without looking over your shoulder at your blindspots. In this nifty book, Payleitner reminds us of the full 360 degree "surround sound" perspective of famous biblical landscapes. Read it, and your scriptural driving will be a lot more fun and safe!

—Dr. Emmett Cooper, author of *The HoneyWord Bible* for kids of all ages; founder and president of HoneyWord Foundation

Tired of fluffy devotions? In a world overcome with the epidemic of Biblical illiteracy, *The Next Verse* is a rich treasure of well-known Scripture presented with fresh, accurate interpretation. So often believers are not taught to study passages within context. But you'll feel like you're having coffee with a friend as Jay unpacks truth in a way anyone can understand. He takes the time to explain topics without heady theological words. Simple, easy exploration of what's been in front of us all the time. I loved it! A must for anyone who desires to be a true student of the Word.

—Tez Brooks, Multiple award-winning author of *The Single Dad Detour* and *Debriefing: Meditations of Hope for Those Who Protect and Serve*

JAY PAYLEITNER

THE

NET

VERSE

WHAT YOU NEVER KNEW ABOUT 60 OF YOUR FAVORITE BIBLE PASSAGES

W

WHITAKER
HOUSE

THE NEXT VERSE:
What You Never Knew About 60 of Your Favorite Bible Passages

jaypayleitner.com

ISBN: 978-1-64123-892-2
eBook 978-1-64123-893-9
Printed in the United States of America
© 2022 by Jay Payleitner

Whitaker House
1030 Hunt Valley Circle
New Kensington, PA 15068
www.whitakerhouse.com

LC record available at https://lccn.loc.gov/2022016253
LC ebook record available at https://lccn.loc.gov/2022016254

1 2 3 4 5 6 7 8 9 10 11 ⨃ 29 28 27 26 25 24 23 22

Introduction

There is no God.

—Psalm 14:1 NLT

Do you know this verse? Actually it's just part of a verse. And when taken by itself, it is totally out of context.

If you tried to pass it off as a complete quote from the Bible, most people would instantly recognize the absurdity of such a blatant untruth. After all, the Bible is God's autobiography. The book's entire purpose is to proclaim His eternal existence and extraordinary attributes.

For the record, the full verse reads, *"Only fools say in their hearts, 'There is no God.' They are corrupt, and their actions are evil; not one of them does good!"* (NLT).

Even an atheist who read the entire verse would discern that the four-word phrase, *"There is no God,"* does not reflect the meaning or intent of the author.

While that statement is easily recognized as misleading, the danger of taking biblical passages out of context is very real. Too many Christians know or recognize small snippets of the Bible but fail to see the big picture. They embrace a biblical concept but neglect to read the surrounding verses and other references that would help them understand the entire scriptural and historical context.

We Christians love to display our favorite verses on plaques, bumper stickers, posters, and framed needlepoint pictures:

"As for me and my house, we will serve the LORD*."*

"Jesus is the way, the truth, and the life."

"Come to me, all of you who are weary and carry heavy burdens, and I will give you rest."[1]

But what about the surrounding verses? What does the entire chapter—not just the single verse—reveal about the nature of God, His purpose for our lives, and all that other good stuff? Let's not be afraid to sweat the details.

Often, right on the same page where we are reading, we can find supporting arguments, corollaries, and deeper truths. On the other hand, sometimes the very next verse seems to say the exact opposite, and that's something that we shouldn't take lightly.

Even worse, it's tempting to elevate the meaning of a short passage that makes us feel good about ourselves or even seems to condone errant behavior. The challenge is to move beyond pithy quotes and easy answers to arrive at solid biblical truth.

So, please: Keep memorizing your favorite verses. Jot them on notecards. Do sword drills with your kids. Write them on your doorposts.

But always, always, always take your favorite passage in context. Together, that's what we'll be doing in the pages ahead with 60 well-known, well-loved verses and passages.

Prepare to be a little surprised. You'll smile and nod your head in recognition of the passage that begins each chapter, but then we'll look at the verses that come next or even before, as well as

---

1. Joshua 24:15 NASB, John 14:6 (paraphrased), Matthew 11:28 NLT

other nearby and related passages that explain, expand, seemingly contradict, or just make you say, "Wow. I hadn't thought of that."

Our goal is to go deeper into the Scriptures and arrive at the ultimate purpose—being transformed into the image of Jesus Christ.

Will you promise yourself this? Before you quote it, cross-stitch it, or leave it on your voicemail, commit to reading *the next verse*.

1

For God so loved the world that he gave
his one and only Son, that whoever believes in him
shall not perish but have eternal life.
—John 3:16

Grace. It's a wonderful, positive message. A message designed to share with the world.

Most of us have never held up a "John 3:16" banner in the end zone of a football stadium. Still, we probably should applaud anyone who does. Who knows what seeds are planted by those evangelists in the bleachers? Who knows how many sports fans have been curious enough to blow the dust off the old family Bible and look up that powerful verse? Between the halves of a college bowl game, it's likely that quite a few lives have been changed forever. The Spirit of God can use all our efforts—even if we're wearing a rainbow wig and waving a "We're #1" foam finger.

The 26 words of John 3:16 have been called "the essence of the Bible." And it's true. This should be one of the first verses we take to heart and the first one we memorize. You have to admit it's a "feel good" verse. The theme is God's love. The proof of His love is that He gave His Son. The message is for the entire world. The promise is eternal life. And all you have to do is believe. It sounds simple. There is no downside.

But keep reading. Consider the next verses:

For God did not send his Son into the world to condemn the world, but to save the world through him. Whoever believes in him is not condemned, but whoever does not believe stands condemned already because they have not believed in the name of God's one and only Son.
—John 3:17–18

Suddenly, we're reading not about grace but about judgment. Why is that? Well, the truth is, you cannot have one without the other. If there were no judgment or condemnation, there would be nothing from which to be saved. Jesus's death would be meaningless. Every man, woman, and child—even wrapped in our sinful nature—would get to sit at the feet of a perfect and holy God. And that's just not possible.

These two verses certainly don't contradict John 3:16. Instead, they are an eye-opening confirmation of just how important grace is to the human condition.

Anyone who turns to verse 16 for hope and comfort should be encouraged to continue reading. Not so that they lose their newfound hope, but so they realize the consequences of not believing. There will be judgment. For some, there will be condemnation. What's more, if the reader is not moved to repent based on the nonspecific concept of God's judgment, then perhaps they should turn to Matthew 13:42 to receive a clearer and more terrifying picture of every person's potential future: *"They will throw them into the blazing furnace, where there will be weeping and gnashing of teeth."*

Finally, worth noting in John 3:18, we read that nonbelievers are *"condemned already."* That seems to indicate that Jesus was sent on a rescue mission. Every person is hell-bound unless and until they put their faith, trust, and confidence in Christ.

The truth is, it's a narrow road. Many men and women will choose the easy path. There is no argument that John 3:16

summarizes the promise of the gospel. But the next two verses may have the best potential for opening the eyes of many lost souls.

GOING DEEPER:

It's amazing how many people can quote John 3:16 but have not really thought much about the intense conversation that led to this grace-affirming verse.

Early in Jesus's ministry, His reputation has already become a problem for the religious leaders when a Pharisee named Nicodemus comes to see Him—in the dark! Jesus has been working miracles around Galilee and Judea, and apparently He's been gaining a reputation as a man who may disrupt the influence and power the Jewish ruling council has over the people.

John chapter three opens with Nicodemus asking legitimate questions about whether Jesus was sent by God and how a man can be born a second time. Was he trying to trap Jesus into saying some kind of blasphemy? It appears not. While Nicodemus does push back with a follow-up question about the Holy Spirit, the conversation begins and ends without any accusations.

Furthermore, Nicodemus later sticks up for Jesus at a council meeting (see John 7), and he even joins Joseph of Arimathea in helping to bury Jesus (see John 19). That's proof of a changed life—from seeking the truth from the living Word.

The simple truth of John 3:16 can be grasped in a moment. Understanding God's plan and the depth of His love takes more than a lifetime.

2

*And we know that in all things God works
for the good of those who love him,
who have been called according to his purpose.*

—Romans 8:28

There is no doubt that Romans 8:28 is a great verse. Memorize it. Cherish the depth of its promise. But please do not quote it out loud at funerals, car accidents, tornado cleanups, cancer diagnosis announcements, or other tragedies.

No doubt it applies in all of the most drastic and dark situations. But anyone who attempts to use Romans 8:28 as words of comfort to a recent widow or a weeping parent should be dragged out behind the barn and severely horsewhipped.

When we are personally suffering from a tragedy and God seems light-years away, this comforting verse, hidden in our hearts, serves as a blessed assurance. There is much strength found in Romans 8:28. To think that God can use our dire circumstance for good is an earth-shattering concept. If and when we embrace that truth and surrender our pain for His purpose, we'll be able to sink into the security of God's outstretched arms even in our darkest hour.

Nevertheless, the last thing a suffering friend, neighbor, or family member needs to hear is a sermon. Especially if they might be a little angry at God because of their pain or on the fence about spiritual matters.

Maybe in a few weeks, at a well-chosen private moment, you can remind them of God's promise to make sense out of sorrow. But, in the short term, the most appropriate biblical response is four chapters later, in Romans 12:15, where Paul writes, *"Rejoice with those who rejoice; mourn with those who mourn."* In other words, instead of preaching or justifying, it is more beneficial to offer a grief-stricken friend a strong shoulder or an open, compassionate heart. In a similar way, Galatians 6:2 challenges us to *"share each other's burdens"* (NLT).

The other challenge that crops up when we take Romans 8:28 out of context is that too many people expect instant answers. When something bad happens, they are quick to ask, "Where is the good?" They analyze and second-guess God's plan. They may not realize that the promise of the verse doesn't guarantee anything in the here and now; it relates to God's purpose and God's timing. And, as everyone knows, to God, a thousand years is like a mere day. (See Psalm 90:4; 2 Peter 3:8.)

Consider carefully the next two verses:

For those God foreknew he also predestined to be
conformed to the image of his Son, that he might
be the firstborn among many brothers and sisters.
And those he predestined, he also called; those he called,
he also justified; those he justified, he also glorified.
—Romans 8:29–30

This passage challenges those who are called to embrace and actually be a part of God's great story, which spans from the beginning of time to the future glory that's waiting for all believers.

The frequent misconception is that the good we anticipate being worked out by God in verse 28 will reflect our own human understanding of good and bad. But the truth is, God's highest priority for each of us is that we be *"conformed to the image* of his Son."* Whatever happens to us, good—as defined by God—will be the ultimate result, but it's going to unfold in His perfect timing, which occurs probably when we least expect it.

A closer look at verses 29 and 30 offers additional clues about God's plan and timing. As believers who have responded to God's call, we are heirs with the Prince! We are Jesus's brothers and sisters, and we are now able to fellowship with our Father in heaven.

Turn to 1 John 3:2. There we find confirmation that anyone who accepts Christ is already a child of God: *"Dear friends, now we are children of God, and what we will be has not yet been made known."* That verse also affirms that the future is both secure and unknown.

Bottom line: we are chosen, called, and promised God's glory. That's not just good—that's the ultimate prize!

GOING DEEPER:

As Christians, we should not only expect good as a result of our suffering, but also actually expect to suffer and—in a very real sense—be grateful for it. Hardship and loss sharpen us, teach us, perfect us, and prepare us to live in glory. You don't have to leave the context of Romans 8 to get this confirmation from verses 17 and 18: *"But if we are to share his glory, we must also share his suffering. Yet what we suffer now is nothing compared to the glory he will give us later"* (NLT). That sounds like a pretty good deal.

> In the end, everything will turn out more than fine, but there are a few reasonable conditions. You need to love God, respond to His call, and seek His will for your life with patience and trust. Then you can count on the good.

3

*An angel of the Lord appeared to him in a dream and said,
"Joseph son of David, do not be afraid to
take Mary home as your wife, because what is conceived in
her is from the Holy Spirit. She will give birth to a son,
and you are to give him the name Jesus,
because he will save his people from their sins."*
—Matthew 1:20–21

In the very first chapter of the New Testament, an angel shows up to provide a confused young carpenter with some stunning insight on how his girlfriend has become pregnant even though she is still a virgin.

Each time I read this passage, I can't help but smile at the tidal wave of emotions Joseph must have been enduring, including fear, wonder, relief, joy, and overall bewilderment. An angel has just visited him with the news that Mary hadn't been cheating on him. The Child had been conceived by the Holy Spirit. But Joseph was going to raise this Child! And his forthcoming Son already had a name and a mission.

These two verses inspire our own anticipation of Christmas! I'm sure you know the story well from the parallel passage of Luke chapter 2: the ninety-mile donkey ride, the inn with no vacancy, the stable, the feeding-trough-turned-crib, the terrified shepherds, and angels filling the night sky.

In addition, Matthew 1:21 spells out the purpose of Jesus's incarnation: *"He will save his people from their sins."* There's a lot packed into that passage.

Like Joseph, are you a bit blown away by the angel's announcement even as you reflect on your own Christmas celebrations as a youth? Or, perhaps, if you're a more recent follower of Christ, you're recalling the many times you saw a nativity scene in front of a church, at a friend's house, or in a Hallmark special, and how, one December, your eyes were opened to finally realize what it all meant.

Admittedly, the first chapter of Matthew—and the second chapter of Luke—provide some of the most iconic, memorable moments in all of Scripture. Discerning the true meaning of Christmas will lead us to envision that newborn three decades into the future—His ministry, miracles, death, and resurrection—and even beyond, acknowledging the way Jesus still touches lives today.

Most certainly, we should hold tight to the future promise of Matthew 1:21, but we should also make sure we don't overlook the critical historical perspective that comes in the next verse.

All this took place to fulfill what the Lord had said through the prophet: "The virgin will conceive and give birth to a son, and they will call him Immanuel" *(which means "God with us").* —Matthew 1:22–23

Fulfilled prophecy proves that Jesus is who He says He is!

For many believers, the purposeful way the Old Testament specifically points to Jesus's life is an important piece of the puzzle they needed to solve before accepting Christ as their personal Savior.

Matthew the Jewish tax collector wisely began his biography of Jesus by reminding his fellow Jews what the prophet Isaiah had written seven hundred years before the birth of Jesus: *"Therefore the Lord himself will give you a sign: The virgin will conceive and give birth to a son, and will call him Immanuel"* (Isaiah 7:14).

GOING DEEPER:

Looking at Matthew's entire gospel, the apostle includes more than a dozen references to prophecies from the Hebrew Bible. Matthew 2:5–6 quotes from Micah that the ruler will come out of Bethlehem. Matthew 3:3 references Malachi and predicts John the Baptist's voice in the wilderness announcing the coming of the Lord. Matthew 13:34–35 confirms the prophecy in Psalm 78 that Jesus would speak in parables. A thoughtful reading of Psalm 22 reveals many parallels to Jesus's crucifixion, including his cry, *"My God, my God, why have you forsaken me?"* (verse 1) as well as the prediction that Jesus's clothes would be divided among the Roman soldiers by casting lots.

Beyond those recounted in the Gospel of Matthew, there are literally hundreds of occurrences in the New Testament that were foretold in the Old Testament. That can't possibly be coincidental.

When it comes to sharing your faith, one effective strategy is to simply tell others what Christ has done in your own life. Another is to describe the rewards of believing in Christ, including the freedom of knowing the truth, guidance from the Holy Spirit, and a reservation in eternity. Some people will respond to Christ because they need a fresh start or an anchor in the storm.

But many seekers require an intellectual approach (or confirmation). Pointing out how Jesus fulfilled hundreds of prophecies written centuries before He was born is a well-founded argument. One you can share at Christmas—or anytime.

Look again at the two contrasting passages highlighted in this short chapter. In one, a heavenly messenger of God brings an incredible miraculous message.
The next two verses point out a simple and logical connection to documented history. That's more proof that the Bible continues to deliver the unexpected.

4

As for me and my family, we will serve the LORD.
—Joshua 24:15 NLT

Moses never made it to the promised land. His handpicked successor would lead the Israelites across the Jordan River and—following clear instructions from God—conquer the land of Canaan. Building a reputation as a brilliant military strategist, Joshua watched the walls of Jericho fall (see Joshua 6) and led the Israelites to conquer a long list of kings (see Joshua 12).

Near the end of his life, Joshua assembles all the tribes of Israel at Shechem. In the last chapter of the Old Testament book bearing his name, the revered leader reminds the people of their history. Joshua 24:1–13 is an extraordinary overview referencing the faithfulness of Abraham, Isaac, Jacob, and Moses. Using God's words, Joshua warns about the dangers of curses and worshipping idols. He urges the Israelites not to forget the struggles that happened even in their own lifetime, including the plagues of Egypt, the escape through the Red Sea, and decades in the desert.

Joshua's farewell is all about making sure the people of Israel know that the victories they achieved came from God, not through their own efforts. He underscores the clear evidence of God's hand every step along the way. Still, Joshua knows humans have short memories. While eager for reassurances that Israel would stay faithful, he doesn't want to hear any hollow promises. His famous speech climaxes with the presentation of a choice the people must make:

> *So fear the* LORD *and serve him wholeheartedly. Put away forever the idols your ancestors worshiped when they lived beyond the Euphrates River and in Egypt. Serve the* LORD *alone. But if you refuse to serve the* LORD, *then choose today whom you will serve. Would you prefer the gods your ancestors served beyond the Euphrates? Or will it be the gods of the Amorites in whose land you now live? But as for me and my family, we will serve the* LORD.   (Joshua 24:14–15 NLT)

The unequivocal response by the gathered crowd is recorded in the next verse:

The people replied,
"We would never abandon the LORD *and serve other gods."*
—Joshua 24:16 NLT

Inspired by their aging leader, the Israelites were undoubtedly sincere in their intentions. But Joshua knew the nature of human weakness, even telling the assembled crowd they would not be able to follow through on their promise and to expect disaster. "No! We will serve the LORD," they insist in verse 24:21. Twice more Joshua challenges them. Twice more they pledge their commitment to God. With that assurance, Joshua makes a covenant for the people and marks the occasion by placing a large stone under an oak tree near the holy place of the Lord.

The final six verses of the book of Joshua describe the burial plot chosen for the leaders of the tribes of Israel in the hill country of Ephraim. Joshua dies at the age of 110, a heroic warrior at peace with the hope that the Israelites are firmly committed to the Lord.

But it doesn't last. A mere two chapters into Judges, the next book in the Old Testament, we find Israel has not kept its promises and has returned to its idolatrous ways. An angel speaks on behalf of the Lord: *"You disobeyed my command. Why did you do this? So now I declare that I will no longer drive out the people living in your land. They will be thorns in your sides, and their gods will be a constant temptation to you"* (Judges 2:2–3 NLT).

GOING DEEPER:

Any study of the Old Testament reveals that God's people— as individuals and as a nation—repeatedly express their devotion to God but then turn away, for any number of reasons. Were their hearts still in Egypt? Did they forget God's Word? Were they spending too much time with pagans and idol worshippers? Were they distracted by prosperity? The answer is: all of the above.

Do you own a Joshua 24:15 plaque, poster, wood carving, or refrigerator magnet? It's a best-seller. You may have posted it publicly as an undeniable statement of faith. But, taken in context, it's not just a pithy statement. It's part of a larger question we need to ask and answer continually about who we choose to follow. A good place to start is remembering God's promise and provision, and protecting yourself from distractions and diversions.

5

Let the one who has never sinned throw the first stone!
—John 8:7 NLT

A woman caught in adultery has broken God's laws. A group of Pharisees brings the woman to the temple courts where a crowd of people has gathered to hear Jesus teach. Their goal is to see if they can trick Jesus into contradicting the law of Moses, which gives clear instruction that the woman should be killed:

> *Suppose a man meets a young woman, a virgin who is engaged to be married, and he has sexual intercourse with her. If this happens within a town, you must take both of them to the gates of that town and stone them to death.*
> (Deuteronomy 22:23–24 NLT)

Jesus knows the law. But He does not condemn her to be stoned. Instead, He quietly and powerfully turns the spotlight on the Pharisees by letting His silence do most of the talking.

> *They put her in front of the crowd. "Teacher," they said to Jesus, "this woman was caught in the act of adultery. The law of Moses says to stone her. What do you say?" They were trying to trap him into saying something they could use against him, but Jesus stooped down and wrote in the dust with his finger.* (John 8:3–6 NLT)

Bible readers have debated for centuries what Jesus may have been drawing in the sand. The sins of the accusers? Their names? The Ten Commandments? Whatever words or images He was tracing, His posture, composure, and quiet solemnity set the tone for an effective lesson in humanity's need for forgiveness and grace.

> *They kept demanding an answer, so he stood up again and said, "All right, but let the one who has never sinned throw the first stone!"* (John 8:7 NLT)

I don't imagine this was a loud "Gotcha!" moment. This Bible translation includes an exclamation mark at the end of Jesus's statement, but I think He would have delivered the words with a quiet, deliberate intensity.

Jesus's rational statement hung in the air as He once again stooped down to write in the dust. One by one, the accusers slipped away from oldest to youngest (see verse 9). The older Pharisees may have been more aware of their own sinful state, or perhaps they realized they had once again been outfoxed by Jesus, underestimating the truth and impact of His words.

In any case, the Pharisees left the scene, leaving behind a lesson for the ages. The lesson is, most of us need to do less judging of others and stay better in tune to our own shortcomings. Beyond that, the incident provides a second lesson that is equally important and even more universal. Sin cannot be ignored, a fact Jesus makes clear in the following verses:

"Where are your accusers? Didn't even one of them condemn you?" "No, Lord," she said. And Jesus said, "Neither do I. Go and sin no more."

—John 8:10–11 NLT

Jesus did not condemn the woman caught in adultery, but He also did not condone her sin. The Bible never tells us whether the woman followed Jesus's instructions, but I like to think a face-to-face intervention with Jesus of Nazareth immediately after being rescued from death by stoning would be a life-changing experience.

We often see in the Gospels that Jesus's goal with sinners seems not to be punishment and condemnation, but rather bringing them to an understanding of their sinful condition and need for a fresh start.

GOING DEEPER:

With all that's happening in this scene from John 8:2–11, it's easy to miss Jesus's brilliant strategy for dealing with conflict. Jesus did not fall into the trap of the scribes and Pharisees. His strategy is one you and I can use. He listened, carefully measured His words, spoke a single thought-provoking sentence, and gave His audience time to think it through.

If you ever feel like you are being pulled into a trap like the one being plotted by the Pharisees, do what it takes to slow down the debate and negotiation. Too often, in tense situations, we rush to judgment or pick up stones to throw. But often the best choice for all involved is to call a time-out, choose our words carefully, and bring calm to the situation. To be sure, Jesus didn't slow things down because He needed time to think. He knew the compelling silence would give the Pharisees time to realize their only chance to save a small shred of dignity was to walk away.

Are you caught in a conflict that feels like it's all going too fast? Does someone in your life need a dose of compassion or forgiveness? Might there be a small secret bundle of your own sins that need to be dealt with? You may want to consider taking the time to stop, lean over, and draw in the sand.

6

For it is by grace you have been saved, through faith—and this is not from yourselves, it is the gift of God—not by works, so that no one can boast.

—Ephesians 2:8–9

Allow me to paraphrase this verse. As imperfect humans, we're all sinners, which means we're not worthy to hang out with God when our time on earth is done. Death is inevitable, and if your sinful condition isn't addressed beforehand, you don't want to imagine how you will be spending eternity.

But fear not. God's perfect and infinite love has provided a solution. He sent His only Son to live perfectly on earth and pay the penalty for our sins on the cross. It cost Him everything. But amazingly, that ticket to heaven costs us nothing. We just have to believe and have faith in His love.

Even when we are sinners, God loves us. There's nothing wonderful or special we can do to earn God's love and nothing terrible that we could do to lose it. We all have different gifts and strengths, and frankly it wouldn't be fair if God's love were dependent on stuff we did or didn't do.

All that to say, grace is a free gift. If it weren't a gift, people would be thinking, *I can do this on my own*, and then crowing about how awesome they are.

Our work doesn't impress God. The Creator of the universe really doesn't need our help.

If you're nodding your head and have accepted the gift, that's a good thing. But don't stop there. Too many believers assume that once you understand the grace described in Ephesians 2:8–9 and your faith kicks in, you can coast through life without too much effort. Those well-meaning folks need to move on to the next verse:

For we are God's handiwork, created in Christ Jesus to do good works, which God prepared in advance for us to do.
—Ephesians 2:10

Hold on! First we read that no work is necessary. Then we read God has been preparing specific work for each and every believer in advance? How does that jibe?

Let's break it down. Because we are God's handiwork, any work we do is really God working through us. He is not leaving us with an insurmountable mountain of tasks to accomplish all by ourselves with no tools.

Second, He has arranged explicit work for us to do for which we have been specifically designed. This is not busywork with no purpose. We have been created to do good works. Our effort will result in direct benefits for others and very likely a dose of personal satisfaction for us.

Third, we should be thrilled to be used by God. We may not know exactly what, where, why, or when. But every believer was created to be an intricate and important part of God's great plan. How cool is that?

Fourth, we shouldn't be surprised that our work is part of God's advanced planning. He exists in all of time and space. We only talk about the idea of God having our work "prepared in advance" because we can't fathom the idea of an eternal being.

Finally—and most importantly—note that salvation *precedes* the assignment. God has indeed prepared work specifically for every new believer, but He doesn't give it to us until after we've experienced regeneration. He saves us, then He equips us each with the specific things we need in order to check off every item on our own personal to-do list.

GOING DEEPER:

After Ephesians 2:8–10 confirms that God has saved us to do good works, Paul spends the rest of the chapter offering an excellent example of the kind of work that needs to be done. That is, building up and bringing peace to the community of believers.

Read for yourself how Christ has destroyed the barrier between people (v. 14), has created a new humanity (v. 15), and preached peace (v. 17).

What's more, God created us not just to do this work, but we ourselves are the work. What a privilege! *"Together, we are his house, built on the foundation of the apostles and the prophets. And the cornerstone is Christ Jesus himself"* (Ephesians 2:20 NLT).

To confirm, if you find yourself working to get God's attention or love or entry into heaven, you're going to fall short. The term "free gift" may be redundant, but it's worth saying because too many people don't understand or forget that grace can't be earned.

7

Come to me, all you who are weary and burdened,
and I will give you rest.
—Matthew 11:28

It's easy to love Matthew 11:28. The message feels like a comforting embrace and delivers a clear instruction that promises reward. "Work hard and then rest." There's even an easygoing lyrical quality to the words of this verse.

We imagine Jesus's voice inviting us to sit in the shade and drink lemonade. Clearly, we've earned our break, having just finished an arduous task. Digging holes for fence posts. Weeding the garden. Painting the back porch. It's time for a well-deserved respite.

"Thanks, J. C.," you say as you mop your brow and kick back in the comfortable Adirondack chair He has provided. The verse suggests enjoying satisfaction in a job well done.

But maybe it's more than that. Maybe your weariness is not from a few hours of sweat-inducing labor, but a real burden that is truly exhausting, not just physically, but mentally, emotionally, and spiritually. Maybe you're suffering desperately from a life challenge that has gripped your very essence and left your soul weary.

Can Jesus help with a boss or bully who makes you feel like crud? Can He provide rest from a financial crisis that seems inescapable? If an ongoing history of abuse, mental illness, addiction, or anything else that is completely out of your control has left you broken, does this verse apply? What if life just doesn't make sense? What if the burden is unexplainable or unspeakable?

What's more, Jesus makes the invitation to "*all you.*" How can He possibly promise that kind of crucial care and comfort to *everyone* who picks up a Bible and reads the Gospel of Matthew?

Might there be answers in the next verse?

Take my yoke upon you and learn from me, for I am gentle and humble in heart, and you will find rest for your souls. For my yoke is easy and my burden is light.
—Matthew 11:29–30

After the promise of Matthew 11:28, the next two verses seem to make no sense. Where's the so-called rest? In the very next verse Jesus introduces the idea of some kind of farm implement we're supposed to strap across our shoulders.

That's right, the primary definition of "yoke" is a wooden collar fitting over the necks of two draft animals, such as oxen or donkeys, joining them to work in tandem to pull a plow, sled, or wagon. Literally, taking on a yoke is pretty much the *opposite* of rest.

Before we call Jesus a liar, let's take a closer look at what He is really recommending for "*all you who are weary and burdened.*" He is not offering just any yoke. He is telling us to take on "*my yoke.*"

Let that sink in. Jesus, the Son of God, is already yoked. He is an expert in taking on heavy loads. He proved that when He took on the burden of sin, including the overwhelming weight of all the sins that were ever committed. In plain language, Matthew 11:29 has the one Divine Being experienced in carrying the weight of the world offering to partner with you. If we come alongside Jesus and share our burden, it's pretty clear that He has the ability to carry all of it.

Confirmation comes in verse 30 and finishes with a promise that being yoked with Jesus leaves us with a challenge that is manageable. He says, *"The burden I give you is light"* (NLT), which means Jesus doesn't give us anything we can't endure. He may give us tremendous responsibilities, but somehow He makes them doable by providing the exact gifts and resources we need to complete them. We can handle the weight. Phew.

GOING DEEPER:

Did you notice the other benefit in this passage? Jesus is offering us the chance to *"learn from me"* (verse 29). As so often happens when we turn to Jesus, He offers the unexpected. He knows working through some challenges is good for us.

Being yoked side-by-side with Jesus gives Him a chance to whisper truths we need to know. While modeling gentleness and humility, He reveals the ready benefits of experiencing affliction. While Jesus provides rest for our souls, He simultaneously gives us a manageable burden that:

+ Confirms our dependence on God
+ Compels us to pray
+ Keeps us humble
+ Sends us into the arms of God
+ Produces endurance
+ Gives us empathy for others in need
+ Reminds us that we are not home yet

These are just a few of the lessons revealed when we turn to Jesus with our heaviest burdens. But only if we let Him teach us.

With all the benefits that come from facing challenges and carrying burdens, is it possible that sometimes we should actually seek them out? Perhaps! At the very least, we can approach each day and each opportunity with a little more courage and confidence knowing that He shares our burden.

8

Be still, and know that I am God.
—Psalm 46:10

When's the last time you were still? Silent. Thoughtful. Contemplative.

Stillness is almost impossible these days. Distractions are constant. We wear busyness as a badge of honor and confuse activity with progress. The loudest voice gets our attention. The squeaky wheel gets the grease. The most obnoxious social media gets shared. Buzzing smartphones beckon us constantly.

Is stillness possible? Go ahead and try twenty seconds of silence right now. If that works, try being still for twenty minutes, twenty hours, or twenty days.

Silence gives us our best chance to recognize God. No doubt, He is in the thunderstorm and crashing waves. But to really know Him and hear His voice requires us to shut out the noise.

A prominent example of stillness prevailing over cacophony can be found during Solomon's rule as Israel's third king. In those days, the prophet Elijah experienced his share of celebrated Old Testament activities such as working miracles, surviving a drought, and representing God in a fiery defeat of the prophets of Baal. Escaping to the desert, the larger-than-life Elijah met the Lord in an unexpected way.

A great and powerful wind tore the mountains apart and shattered the rocks before the Lord, *but the* Lord *was not in the wind. After the wind there was an earthquake, but the* Lord *was not in the earthquake. After the earthquake came a fire, but the* Lord *was not in the fire. And after the fire came a gentle whisper.*   (1 Kings 19:11–12)

The quiet conversation that followed required Elijah to recognize the formidable presence and clarity in the whispered voice of God.

Stillness is not a typical theme in Psalms. You can find a few other short passages that recommend silence, listening, and peace, but in general this book in the middle of the Old Testament is filled with a wide range of audible distractions—music, proclamations, righteous pleas, and exaltations to the Lord.

With that in mind, after reading *"Be still, and know that I am God,"* we are brought back to exalting God in the second half of that verse:

I will be exalted among the nations,
I will be exalted in the earth.
—Psalm 46:10

So in our quest to know God and honor Him, should we choose to be silent or to exalt? You may be surprised to know that exalting doesn't necessarily require increased volume. Any dictionary definition suggests it has more to do with honoring and elevating in rank. So, let's commit to doing both—offering God the elevation and honor He deserves both with louder activities and with contemplation.

Quiet exaltation. Knowing God and being at peace. That sounds pretty good, especially when you consider a few other passages found in Psalm 46.

God is our refuge and strength, an ever-present help in trouble. Therefore we will not fear, though the earth give way and the mountains fall into the heart of the sea, though its waters roar and foam and the mountains quake with their surging.
(Psalm 46:1–3)

Nations are in uproar, kingdoms fall; he lifts his voice, the earth melts.   (Psalm 46:6)

Come and see what the LORD *has done, the desolations he has brought on the earth.*   (Psalm 46:8)

Futurists suggest that the idea of the seas foaming, mountains quaking, the earth melting, and desolations brought by God portend the inevitability of nuclear war. The psalmist actually paints a pretty bleak (and some say accurate) picture of today's world.

That idea should be frightening for those who don't know God. But Psalm 46 ends with the assurance that we can know God and He will continue to protect His chosen people.

He says, "Be still, and know that I am God; I will be exalted among the nations, I will be exalted in the earth." The LORD *Almighty is with us; the God of Jacob is our fortress.*
(Psalm 46:10–11)

When will God "lift His voice," allowing the earth to melt? Maybe in our lifetime. Maybe He already has. Maybe the psalmist is writing symbolically. No matter how or when, God's victory is assured. Let's assume we will be standing in awe at that time in stillness and assurance that God is God.

GOING DEEPER:

In life, the greatest value in standing still may be that our hearing greatly improves. The hunter tracking his prey stops to listen. The coach blows her whistle, gathers the team, and gains their full attention before speaking. The husband who truly cares about his wife will put down his phone, turn off SportsCenter, and even shift his entire body in her direction to hear her heart.

Let's all pledge to spend a little more time in stillness and listen with a bit more intentionality. Romans 10:17 confirms how important that is, especially to those who want to have an authentic belief: *"Faith comes from hearing."*

It may seem like being still comes from ignorance or hesitation about what the right thing to do is. Actually, it's just the opposite. We choose to be still because we know we are part of a bigger picture. We humbly know we have much to learn. We want to take it all in. To listen. To see. To think through our best options. To hear the whisper of God.

9

*He who began a good work in you will carry it on to
completion until the day of Christ Jesus.*
—Philippians 1:6

Let's dedicate this chapter to all the procrastinators out there.
This verse and the next verse also apply nicely to any new believers who are not exactly sure how the idea of surrendering their
life to Jesus and following Him is going to work out. As we look
at Philippians 1:6–7, we'll also include some appreciation for
established Christians who are overflowing with God's grace and
eagerly reflect that supernatural love in their lives.

Here we go. If you happen to be a sluggish, dawdling laggard,
I would recommend you bookmark and underline Philippians 1:6
in your Bible. The verse might inspire you to make sure the work
you are planning is *"good work"* and—if so—to realize that God
will give you every opportunity to complete it. But don't dawdle
too long because you could be meeting Jesus tomorrow—when He
returns or if you happen to fall off a cliff.

A closer look at Philippians 1:6 in context reveals that Paul is
writing to the church at Philippi to encourage them—not in mundane worldly pursuits—but in their modestly successful efforts
spreading the gospel. The promise that our good work will lead to
a fruitful harvest still applies today.

God's work on our behalf began on the cross and continues in our lives as we accept grace, trust Him, follow Jesus's teaching, and listen to the Holy Spirit. Once we begin our journey of faith, the work of the entire Trinity is going to make sure our work is finished at just the right time—in God's timing, not ours.

It really doesn't get any better than that. God is on our side, helping us finish the race. But there's also undeniable value in having human brothers and sisters in Christ rooting for us. Paul himself volunteers to be your cheerleader in the next verse:

It is right for me to feel this way about all of you,
since I have you in my heart and, whether I am
in chains or defending and confirming the gospel,
all of you share in God's grace with me.
—Philippians 1:7

Writing from prison, Paul has written this letter primarily to say, "Good job!" and "Keep at it!" In their entirety, the four chapters of Philippians radiate with the idea of rejoicing in the Lord as we serve, share, persevere through struggles, and press on toward the goal. At one point, Paul even tells the Philippians that they are on track to *"shine…like stars in the sky"* (Philippians 2:15).

Paul's words are intentional. In Philippians 1:6–7, he confirms God's promise to make sure we successfully finish the race and then adds his own human pat on the back and shot on the arm. He is writing from prison *"in chains"* and yet is still committed to *"defending and confirming the gospel."* Best of all, he reaffirms that he is in partnership with everyone who reads this letter, which includes you and me today. We are in his heart and sharing God's grace.

GOING DEEPER:

Reading and rereading Philippians 1:6–7 (and maybe the entire letter) may be more productive than buying any self-help book, listening to a motivational speaker, or visiting your therapist.

Are you feeling apathetic? God will give you inspiration to finish every good task. Are you unsure of your calling as a believer? Take one step in any direction, and God will reveal whether you're headed the right way by clearing that path and helping you carry your work to completion.

In addition, this passage is a valuable tool for parents, bosses, pastors, and teachers. You're now equipped the next time someone in your charge says, "I can't do this," "I'll never get this done," or "I should have never started this." As a mentor or leader, feel free to use the biblical admonitions, "God began this, and He will continue to work in you and through you." Maybe try, "Finish the race," "Fight the good fight," or "Keep the faith." Even add your own commitment, telling them, "Win or lose, you can count on me to be cheering you on along with our heavenly Father."

Pause for a moment. Who do you know who could use a word of encouragement? It doesn't have to be someone within earshot, and you don't have to be in optimal condition yourself. Paul was in prison while writing this letter, but he still filled it with reasons to rejoice. If the Philippians saw the return address on that scroll, they would have been double honored. Wow! Paul is stuck in prison and he's telling them to rejoice. They were likely blown away.

Taking that idea one step further, being a cheerleader for someone else may be the exact tonic you need to get out of the doldrums and take your mind off your own woes.

10

Jesus answered, "I am the way, the truth, and the life. No one can come to the Father except through me."
—John 14:6 NLT

Remember Thomas, the apostle who was absent the first time Jesus appeared to the disciples after the resurrection? When the other disciples told him they had seen the Lord, Thomas replied, *"Unless I see the nail marks in his hands and put my finger where the nails were, and put my hand into his side, I will not believe"* (John 20:25).

Before we disparage that apostle as "Doubting Thomas," let's consider his thought process. Healthy doubt is actually a good thing. It simply means you haven't made up your mind yet. Doubt leads to asking good questions. Working through a bit of skepticism produces personal conviction about what and why you believe. Doubts, once they're answered, produce courage, conviction, and ammunition to share your faith.

As it turns out, a week later, Thomas's doubts were removed when Jesus once again appeared in the upper room behind locked doors and told Thomas, *"Put your finger here; see my hands. Reach out your hand and put it into my side. Stop doubting and believe"* (John 20:27).

Why are we talking about Thomas in this chapter? That dramatic scene in the upper room took place after Jesus's death and resurrection and secured Thomas's place in biblical history. But a different question he asked weeks earlier led to an equally startling realization for the disciples and for us today.

In John 14:5, Thomas asks Jesus for directions to heaven! Confessing confusion, he asks, *"Lord, we don't know where you are going, so how can we know the way?"*

Jesus expresses the puzzling idea that He Himself is *"the way, the truth, and the life."* Aware that such a claim could be confusing to the disciples, Jesus continues with the next verse:

If you had really known me, you would know who my Father is. From now on, you do know him and have seen him!
—John 14:7 NLT

Still confused? So were the apostles. The remainder of John chapter 14 features Jesus answering additional questions from the disciples, including Philip and Judas (not Judas Iscariot).

Jesus explains—not for the first time—that *"I am in the Father and the Father is in me"* (v. 11). In addition, Jesus provides insight on what life will be like after He ascends into heaven, describing how the disciples will do great things and how the Father will send the Holy Spirit to be another Counselor (see verses 12–16).

Additional passages later in the New Testament articulate other ways to describe the mystery of how God and Jesus are one. Colossians 1:15 says, *"The Son is the image of the invisible God, the firstborn over all creation."* Hebrews 1:3 confirms, *"The Son is the radiance of God's glory and the exact representation of his being."*

GOING DEEPER:

So you don't miss it, two of the greatest truths of Scripture are brought to life in John 14:6–7:

- Know Jesus, and you will know God.

- Jesus is the only way to heaven.

The first truth cancels any idea that Jesus is not fully God. The second truth will not sit well with a lot of folks who suggest that there are multiple paths to heaven.

You can't go any deeper than that.

John 20:24 tells us Thomas was nicknamed "the Twin." Since there is no other mention of a twin brother, theologians aren't exactly sure why the Bible tells us of Thomas's nickname. Who and where is that doubting twin? I have a hunch it might be me. Or you.

11

*For those who exalt themselves will be humbled, and those
who humble themselves will be exalted.*
—Matthew 23:12

With words that may have come as a surprise to the disciples, Matthew 23 begins with Jesus displaying a dose of respect for the title and role held by the Pharisees and teachers of the law. Jesus tells the gathered crowd that since they sit in the seat of Moses, *"you must be careful to do everything they tell you"* (Matthew 23:3).

Then in the same verse He quickly clarifies how He sees the religious leaders. Perhaps without changing tone, He continues to teach: *"But do not do what they do, for they do not practice what they preach"* (v. 3). Jesus provides examples of their hypocrisy, including the way they dress, the way they put on airs, the way they seek out places of honor at banquets and synagogues, and how they love their titles and being fawned over in the marketplace (see verses 5–7).

Jesus then delivers another thoughtful, direct assertion that would have left some members of the crowd puzzled: *"The greatest among you will be your servant. For those who exalt themselves will be humbled, and those who humble themselves will be exalted"* (Matthew 23:11–12).

His demeanor then changes. Jesus is no longer addressing His disciples or those who are eager for His teaching. He addresses the

Pharisees who may or may not be within earshot. Perhaps Jesus has spotted a tasseled garment in the crowd, its wearer grimacing in defiance. Or maybe He simply wants to make it clear that self-centered religion and false piety are not the pathway to eternal life.

You can imagine Jesus shifting from teacher to judge—from composure to rage—in the next verse:

Woe to you, teachers of the law and Pharisees,
you hypocrites! You shut the door of the kingdom of heaven
in people's faces. You yourselves do not enter,
nor will you let those enter who are trying to.
—Matthew 23:13

The righteous anger displayed by Jesus is not short-lived. In the following extended passage, He confronts the religious hypocrites seven times with the words, *"Woe to you…"* He charges them with a list of sins, including blocking the way to heaven, recruiting converts for corrupt purposes, and neglecting justice and mercy. Jesus compares them to whitewashed tombs and to cups clean on the outside but dirty on the inside. He calls them snakes and murderers. (See verses 13–29.) It is no surprise that most Bible translations load those verses with exclamation points.

This entire passage, an unbroken speech filled with graphic and gripping imagery, should get the attention of any Bible reader today. What's more, it's easy to join Jesus in judgment of these Pharisees and teachers of the law. But the more valuable application found in this passage may be a personal challenge to today's readers. That is to look within our own hearts and be convicted of even a small hint of blindness, false piety, or hypocrisy.

GOING DEEPER:

Popular culture has this image of Jesus being a really sweet guy who would never be judgmental and rarely expresses anger. But that's not the Jesus of the Bible. The Son of God took a stand when it came to sinners, blasphemers, and those who would divert His earthly mission.

Beyond Matthew 23:13–36, we can find several examples. Jesus warned those who would bring harm to a child, *"It would be better for them to be thrown into the sea with a millstone tied around their neck than to cause one of these little ones to stumble"* (Luke 17:2). When Jesus predicted His own death, Peter protested the plan and was strongly rebuked, *"Get behind me, Satan!"* (Mark 8:33).

Jesus's most public and notable recorded outburst was all about the corrupt emphasis on materialism. Merchants and moneychangers had set up shop in the temple, charging exorbitant fees and crowding out those who came to worship.

Jesus entered the temple courts and drove out all who were buying and selling there. He overturned the tables of the money changers and the benches of those selling doves. "It is written," he said to them, "'My house will be called a house of prayer,' but you are making it 'a den of robbers.'"

(Matthew 21:12–13)

Of course, there are other Scripture passages that warn about the dangers of anger. But most of those verses tend to warn about foolish anger, having a quick temper, or allowing anger to lead you to actions you regret.

Ephesians 4:26 sums up the challenge, suggesting anger is not the problem. The goal is learning to handle anger judiciously and righteously: *"In your anger do not sin."*

Revisiting the verse that launched this discussion, it appears a good goal would be to live with humility because it leads to being exalted. If you ever find yourself in a boastful, prideful, egocentric mood, you would do well to open your Bible to Galatians 6:14: "May I never boast except in the cross of our Lord Jesus Christ, through which the world has been crucified to me, and I to the world."

12

For the word of God is alive and powerful. It is sharper than the sharpest two-edged sword.
—Hebrews 4:12 NLT

There's power in God's living Word. John's gospel opens with a memorable description of the Word being with God, of God, and from God. The Word is eternal. And the Word was made flesh in the coming of Jesus. (See John 1:1–5, 14.)

That's a lot to take in. In the dramatic description of the "Armor of God" in Ephesians chapter 6, the Bible is nicknamed "the sword of the spirit." In the above verse, the author of Hebrews further imagines the Word of God as a powerful living sword with two razor-sharp blades.

That sword is a weapon we, as Christians, sometimes grasp in both hands to brandish against our enemies. We imagine ourselves as a swashbuckling hero correcting others of their heinous thoughts and behavior. It's exhilarating.

Another favorite passage describes the practicality of the Bible equipping us and seemingly giving us permission to take up that sword and use it to teach, rebuke, correct, and train others.

All Scripture is God-breathed and is useful for teaching, rebuking, correcting and training in righteousness, so that the

> *servant of God may be thoroughly equipped for every good*
> *work.*   (2 Timothy 3:16–17)

We especially love to imagine the glistening blades striking fear into our enemies.

But the funny thing about a two-edged sword is that, while you're slicing into your neighbor, exposing their sins, the other edge of that sword is facing back at you. Consider the second half of Hebrews 4:12:

...cutting between soul and spirit, between joint and marrow.
It exposes our innermost thoughts and desires.
—Hebrews 4:12 NLT

Upon further examination, Hebrews 4:12 and 2 Timothy 3:16–17 don't say anything about our enemies. When we read God's Word and take it to heart, our own innermost thoughts and desires are exposed—not those of our enemies. As it turns out, we are the ones who are being taught, rebuked, corrected, and trained in righteousness.

Did you see that coming? Many Christians are eager to wield the Bible as a weapon against their fellow humans. But when the Sword of the Spirit cuts between our own soul and spirit, we often don't like what's revealed. That's why we need to keep reading the Bible in its entirety and continue to apply it to our lives.

Anyone can read the Bible, but its message is most readily applicable to believers. When an atheist reads Scripture, it's as if they are reading someone else's mail.

GOING DEEPER:

What does Hebrews 4:12 mean by *"cutting between soul and spirit"*? And how does that slashing blade expose our hidden thoughts?

As described in the closing verses of 1 Thessalonians, believers have three interwoven realities—body, soul, and spirit.

Now may the God of peace make you holy in every way, and may your whole spirit and soul and body be kept blameless until our Lord Jesus Christ comes again.

(1 Thessalonians 5:23 NLT)

The body is our physical self here on earth, which is fairly easy to identify. It's the temporary part of us that experiences the physical senses. The soul lasts for eternity, and everyone has one. We feel emotions—love, hate, anger, jealousy, gratitude, awe, horror, sympathy—in our soul. The Spirit is a member of the Trinity, a gift received when believers are born again uniting them with Christ, and it communes with our spirit.

The sharpened blade of God's Word doesn't literally cut into our bodies. It also wouldn't wound the Holy Spirit, the very source of new life within us. But the Bible—God's law and the Sword of the Spirit—can and does disclose the condition of our soul, exposing our sinful condition and our need for a Savior. As it cuts, it reveals where our soul is at odds with the Holy Spirit. As confirmed in Romans 3:20, *"Through the law we become conscious of our sin."* That knowledge and awareness is an important reminder as we continually surrender our will to Christ.

> **Reading Scripture exposes your innermost thoughts, leaving you with two choices. Look the other way or be convicted and work toward making the necessary changes.**
> **Your best life awaits you if you allow that double-edged sword to do its work.**

13

I can do all this through him who gives me strength.
—Philippians 4:13

You've surely seen an inspiring poster quoting Philippians 4:13. Most often it is quoted as "I can do all things through him who gives me strength," combining a few Bible versions of the verse. A recent web search for wall art inspired by that verse yielded 539,000 results. Often hanging in weight rooms, man caves, and bedrooms, these posters include images of sweating athletes, gravity-defying mountain climbers, and lots of dramatic close-up photos of sports gear.

You've got to applaud parents who give those kinds of posters to their sports-minded sons and daughters. It's a youth-friendly way to acknowledge that the Bible is more than just a book of rules. The verse suggests that God provides the power for an athlete to give 110 percent and maybe even do the impossible. Encouraging boys and girls to finish strong and do great things, Philippians 4:13 is undeniably inspiring.

But how does one get to that point of empowerment? An even better question is, "Can I really do *all* things?" Let's take a look at the previous verse:

*I know what it is to be in need, and I know what it is
to have plenty. I have learned the secret of being content in
any and every situation, whether well fed or hungry,
whether living in plenty or in want.*
—Philippians 4:12

Before Paul makes the audacious claim that he "can do all things," he reveals that he has learned a valuable secret—how to be "*content in any and every situation.*" This insight suggests that Paul has discovered the ability to discern what's really important. It's not about lavish meals or having lots of stuff. It's not about climbing mountains or winning football games. It's about rejoicing in the Lord.

Just a few verses back—Philippians 4:4—Paul even writes, "*Rejoice in the Lord always. I will say it again: Rejoice!*"

He gained this perspective and learned this secret the hard way, by escaping death more times than we can count. Several times, angry mobs tried to stone him. Once he was left for dead. Paul was bitten by a poisonous snake, robbed, thrown in jail several times, shipwrecked three times, and spent a whole night adrift at sea. He survived floods, starvation, and five separate whippings. (See 2 Corinthians 11:16–33.) Despite these trials—or maybe because of them—he still rejoiced in the Lord.

One clear lesson is that if you endure enough adversity you begin to realize what's really important. Paul knew the strength allowing him to survive came from God. What's more, Paul wasn't afraid to die. He even wrote, "*To live is Christ and to die is gain*" (Philippians 1:21).

Ultimately, God would use Paul to reach the gentiles, encourage and challenge churches, write much of the New Testament, and be an example for how to set our priorities on eternal matters.

GOING DEEPER:

In one way, all those posters that quote Philippians 4:13 and cheer on athletes to dig deep and achieve greatness because they are receiving strength from the Creator are misleading. The verse leading up to Philippians 4:13 isn't about digging deep to be better, faster, stronger, or more successful. It's about searching deep in your heart to be content with any circumstance in which you find yourself.

If you're a coach or a parent, that might seem to be the opposite of what you want to tell a young athlete. But think again. The Christian life is about finding contentment in your role as a disciple. That requires being committed to discipline. Keeping your eyes on the prize. Putting others before yourself. Seeing the bigger picture. Living your life as a testimony to others. Modeling excellence. Making sure not to waste your efforts needlessly. Being ready for the next challenge. Earning the prize that waits for every believer at the end of our earthly lives. Those are all qualities found in world-class athletes.

Those goals are also reflected in another popular passage that sometimes finds its way onto motivational posters. Paul wrote these words in his first letter to the church at Corinth.

Do you not know that in a race all the runners run, but only one gets the prize? Run in such a way as to get the prize. Everyone who competes in the games goes into strict training. They do it to get a crown that will not last, but we do it to get a crown that will last forever. Therefore I do not run like someone running aimlessly; I do not fight like a boxer beating the air. No, I strike a blow to my body and make it my slave so that after I have preached to others, I myself will not be disqualified for the prize. (1 Corinthians 9:24–27)

The truth is that believers *can* do anything and everything that matters through Christ who provides the strength. Winning that race will gain you a prize worthy of your sacrificial devotion.

Are you dedicating your life to earning a crown that rusts and doesn't last? Or are you pursuing a crown that will last forever? That's where you'll find joy and purpose here on earth while qualifying for the ultimate prize in the world to come.

14

To act justly and to love mercy and
to walk humbly with your God.
—Micah 6:8

I had to include this verse in this devotional. In our family room is a lovely piece of framed art with an abridged version of Micah 6:8. It says simply, "Act justly. Love mercy. Walk humbly." That's good stuff, right?

To be honest, I've been looking at those six words for several years and never really took the time to consider the context and application. So it turns out, I'm writing this chapter mostly for me.

The book of Micah is only seven chapters, 105 verses. The minor prophet spends much of those chapters delivering well-deserved judgment on Israel and Judah for corrupt leadership and idolatry. In Micah's time, King Ahaz had set up pagan idols and nailed the temple doors shut. (See 2 Chronicles 28:22–24.) Of course, it would never happen today, but back then empty displays of religion were commonplace as preachers pursued personal wealth and influence. (That's sarcasm, folks.) Micah goes on to point out these sins and charges the religious and political leaders with fraud, murder, hating good, and loving evil, and he predicts the Lord's judgment and destruction.

All is not lost, however, because in the midst of calling out God's people for their injustice, Micah offers two avenues for hope at the end of the book by delivering a promising message. As the Old Testament has revealed over and over again, God's faithfulness cannot be denied. Israel will confess its sin and find forgiveness, restoration, and blessing.

Tucked into chapter five is the even more hopeful and inspiring promise of the coming Messiah: *"But you, Bethlehem Ephrathah, though you are small among the clans of Judah, out of you will come for me one who will be ruler over Israel, whose origins are from of old, from ancient times"* (Micah 5:2).

In that context, Micah delivers a three-part directive *"to act justly and to love mercy and to walk humbly with your God."* Those specific instructions are actually a response to five questions that make up the previous verses:

With what shall I come before the LORD and bow down before the exalted God? Shall I come before him with burnt offerings, with calves a year old? Will the LORD be pleased with thousands of rams, with ten thousand rivers of olive oil? Shall I offer my firstborn for my transgression, the fruit of my body for the sin of my soul? He has shown you, O mortal, what is good. And what does the LORD require of you?

—Micah 6:6–8

These are the kind of questions that come up time and again in the Old Testament, especially when an individual or entire nation messes up. *We hereby acknowledge our sins. What sacrifices are required by law to make amends?*

These questions demonstrate that sacrificing calves, rams, olive oil, and even firstborn sons were routine transactions between God and man. In most cases, the sacrifice did not come with any regret or apology. They agreed to *"bow down before the exalted God,"* but there was no brokenness or authentic repentance. In many ways, as long as the people were willing to make an occasional sacrificial offering, they had no reason to stop sinning! No wonder the people continued to turn their backs on God and return over and over again to idols and their evil ways.

With the foretelling that a ruler would be born in Bethlehem, Micah confirms his role as a prophet by giving us a taste of what's coming in the New Testament. Jesus will pay the price for all the sins of the world. The Son of God is the ultimate sacrificial lamb. Humans can no longer buy our way out of sin. God doesn't want a transaction; He wants a relationship. That's why Micah was given the privilege of predicting the coming Messiah. And that's why Micah also gave us that three-part instruction in Micah 6:8.

In many ways, it's much easier to burn a calf than to act with justice, be merciful, and walk humbly with God.

GOING DEEPER:

Breaking down that three-part directive of Micah 6:8 requires us to do more than just check off three boxes. We have to change our hearts.

To act justly requires us to discern right and wrong, delve into the motivations that lead to sin, and acknowledge how sin breaks God's heart. Acting with justice means evil must be punished. But it also depends on the existence of a moral code that applies to all humankind in all situations. Psalm 37:28 tells us, *"For the* LORD *loves justice, and he will never abandon the godly. He will keep them safe forever, but the children of the wicked will die"* (NLT).

To love mercy is the flip side of the same coin. Evil must be punished, but a merciful God gifted us with Jesus's sacrificial work on the cross. In the same way, we need to show mercy—pardoning as we have been pardoned. Matthew 5:7 reminds us in the Beatitudes, *"Blessed are the merciful, for they will be shown mercy."*

To walk humbly with God creates an image that should resonate with all believers. The biblical records suggest that only two men literally walked with God: Enoch (see Genesis 5:24) and Noah (see Genesis 6:9). While that is hard to imagine, the idea of drawing close to God and feeling His presence should be well-grounded with those who have received Christ as Savior. Being guided by the Holy Spirit and following the truths of Scripture will not keep you in step with God's exact footsteps—we will still sin—but you'll always be on the right path. After all, Galatians 5:16 says we can *"walk by the Spirit,"* and Psalm 119:105 confirms that *"Your word is a lamp for my feet, a light on my path."*

Act justly. Love mercy. Walk humbly with God. Before you post those precepts on your wall, consider the promise that you're making. Of course, we all fall short of God's glory. We can't keep up with God's infinite strides. But you can draw near Him, and He promises to draw near to you. (See James 4:8.)

15

Man shall not live on bread alone, but on every word that comes from the mouth of God.
—Matthew 4:4, quoting Deuteronomy 8:3

In the time between His baptism and the beginning of His earthly ministry, Jesus was led by the Holy Spirit to spend 40 days and nights fasting in the desert. Although He was fully God, Jesus endured the experience as a human. Satan saw his chance to tempt the Son of God, not knowing he was actually opening the door to a lesson that would empower Christians for centuries to come.

As a man, Jesus would be hungry. Just like us. As a man, Jesus would be tempted. Just like us. Satan saw that human weakness in Jesus and offered Him an easy way out, saying, *"If you are the Son of God, tell these stones to become bread"* (Matthew 4:3).

Jesus could have done exactly that. He could have called angels to deliver a bag of cheeseburgers or a full seven-course meal. But instead—as a man—Jesus modeled for us the most powerful way to deal with Satan's tempting with something we can all do. Jesus responded by quoting the Bible.

In its entirety, Matthew 4:4 says, *"Jesus answered, 'It is written: "Man shall not live on bread alone, but on every word that comes from the mouth of God."'"*

You may be wondering what part of Scripture Jesus was quoting. Most Bibles provide a footnote that cross-references

Deuteronomy 8:3, which takes us back to the words of Moses just before the Israelites enter the promised land. In that last book of the Pentateuch, Moses had a message of remembrance and instruction for God's people. He was well aware that the journey from Egypt to the Jordan River could have taken a matter of days, but instead they wandered in the desert for 40 years. There, on the east side of the river, in sight of Canaan, Moses gave a much-needed history lesson of how God had liberated Israel from slavery and then he reviewed the laws that set apart the people of Israel, including the Ten Commandments. Here's how chapter 8 of Deuteronomy begins:

> *Be careful to follow every command I am giving you today, so that you may live and increase and may enter and possess the land the LORD promised on oath to your ancestors. Remember how the LORD your God led you all the way in the wilderness these forty years, to humble and test you in order to know what was in your heart, whether or not you would keep his commands. He humbled you, causing you to hunger and then feeding you with manna, which neither you nor your ancestors had known, to teach you that man does not live on bread alone but on every word that comes from the mouth of the LORD.* (Deuteronomy 8:1–3)

In His youth, Jesus would have read these words of Moses in the Torah and embraced this history. He understood the Bible was nourishment for the soul. His emphatic response to Satan's desert temptation was based on the knowledge and trust of God's provision, which is the same knowledge and trust we have today.

That day in the desert, Satan would try twice more to tempt Jesus. Twice more Jesus would respond by quoting Deuteronomy in subsequent verses:

Do not put the Lord your God to the test.
—Matthew 4:7, quoting Deuteronomy 6:16

Worship the Lord your God, and serve him only.
—Matthew 4:10, quoting Deuteronomy 6:13

Jesus was weak from hunger, but He still chose to withhold the use of His divine power, confident that the power of the Word would gain victory over the tempter. Jesus's final command that day is one we can also use: *"Away from me, Satan!"* (Matthew 4:10).

You have to love the next verse: *"Then the devil left him, and angels came and attended him"* (v. 11).

GOING DEEPER:

Being tempted is not a sin. Jesus lived a sinless life, but He endured face-to-face temptation from the Father of Lies, who was using every trick in the book. As humans seeking to please God, we may feel like we have disappointed Him when we are tempted to sin. But take heart. God knows we will be tempted. It's how we *respond* that matters. He created us with free will, and He is well aware that sometimes we'll fail. Matthew 26:41 warns, *"Watch and pray so that you will not fall into temptation. The spirit is willing, but the flesh is weak."*

Still, we should use every tool in our arsenal to flee temptation. That includes choosing who we hang out with, where we go, what we put in our bodies, and what we take into our minds, and submitting ourselves to God: *"Submit yourselves, then, to God. Resist the devil, and he will flee from you"* (James 4:7).

Hebrews 2:18 confirms that Jesus allowed Himself to be hungry and tempted in the desert as a model for all of us: *"Because he himself suffered when he was tempted, he is able to help those who are being tempted.*" Looking back at that scenario in the Judean desert, Jesus may have demonstrated the most powerful tool we have, internalizing and speaking God's Word. The knowledge of Scripture equips us to say, *"Away from me, Satan!"*

Satan uses the same temptation today that he tried to use with Jesus 2,000 years ago: appealing to our physical needs, our pride, and our desire for power. You've been warned but, after carefully considering the first 11 verses of Matthew 4, hopefully now you're also well equipped to resist.

16

Do to others as you would have them do to you.
—Luke 6:31

The Golden Rule. You know it well. The world knows it well. Or do they? You may have heard the claim that all the world's major religions preach some version of the Golden Rule and therefore all religions are pretty much the same.

Indeed, search through other religious writings and you'll find phrases that do sound similar:

> Confucianism says, "Do not do to others what you would not like yourself" (Analect 12:2).

> Buddhism says, "Hurt not others in ways that you yourself would find hurtful" (Udana-Varga 5:18).

> Hinduism says, "One should never do that to another which one regards as injurious to one's own self" (Anusasana Parva 113:8).

Further examination reveals that these three examples are stated in the negative. Those religions seem to be more concerned with what *not* to do than what their followers *should* do. The positive proactive command of Luke 6:31 in God's Holy Bible is very much in keeping with much of Jesus's teaching.

Jesus turned the world upside down with the idea of loving your enemies and praying for those who persecute you. Going the extra mile for those who would do you harm is exemplified in Matthew 5:40–42:

> *If anyone wants to sue you and take your shirt, hand over your coat as well. If anyone forces you to go one mile, go with them two miles. Give to the one who asks you, and do not turn away from the one who wants to borrow from you.*

This is all part of the ongoing theme in the Gospels to "Love your neighbor." Except here in Luke chapter 6, Jesus takes it another whole step. Notice, He's not saying which neighbors to love. Because, frankly, it's easy to love the nice neighbors with the cute kids who bring you Christmas cookies and invite you over for burgers on the grill. But what about those neighbors who blast music all night, toss beer bottles on your lawn, or put up campaign signs for candidates of the "other" party? Do you—can you—love them?

As you're debating how you are going to apply the Golden Rule, you may want to take a look at the next verses:

> *If you love those who love you, what credit is that to you?*
> *Even sinners love those who love them.*
> *And if you do good to those who are good to you,*
> *what credit is that to you? Even sinners do that.*
> —Luke 6:32–33

Most people see the Golden Rule as a standalone statement. They never read the logical expansion offered here. Jesus is saying that doing good to those who are good to you is not heroic at all. He seems to finish that thought with a sigh, "*Even sinners do that.*"

Please note, Jesus is not dismissing the Golden Rule. He's simply making sure that the disciples and future believers don't take the easy way out. We should do good to those who do good to us *and* those who don't.

GOING DEEPER:

If the above revelations inspire you, you may want to consider more positive ways to implement the Golden Rule. Scroll down to Luke 6:35: *"Love your enemies, do good to them, and lend to them without expecting to get anything back. Then your reward will be great, and you will be children of the Most High."*

Suddenly, you're not just enduring your nasty neighbor, you're truly loving them: doing good on their behalf and even lending them power tools or toilet plungers without expecting them back. Don't do it because you expect a return, but if I'm reading Luke 6:35 right, one outcome just happens to be that *"your reward will be great."*

One final biblical challenge you might consider is even more difficult because we all like to get credit for the good things we do.

> *When you give to the needy, do not let your left hand know what your right hand is doing, so that your giving may be in secret. Then your Father, who sees what is done in secret, will reward you.*   (Matthew 6:3–4)

Although your act of kindness comes with the promise of some kind of accolade or compensation, there's a high likelihood you may not receive your reward until you're home in heaven. But if you think about it, that's not a bad deal. Rather than receive temporary accolades here on earth for your good works, wouldn't it be extra cool to do your good work in secret and receive that reward in the eternal world to come?

You now have a reasonable and knowledgeable response if you ever hear someone say, "All religions are the same. They all have the Golden Rule." With confidence you can say, "I've heard that before. But actually, the wording is quite different. In the Bible, the Golden Rule is stated as a positive way to love your neighbor. With the other world religions, it has a negative spin, almost more like a warning."

17

Do not judge, or you too will be judged.
—Matthew 7:1

It has been said that Matthew 7:1 is the most misused verse in all of Scripture. If you challenge someone regarding a clear sin in their life, there's a high probability they are going to respond with something like, "Don't judge me. The Bible says, 'Judge not.'"

You know what? They might be right. Because if the person you are confronting is not an authentic Christian, then your words will fall on deaf ears. You may be able to clearly see their sinful choices, but we shouldn't expect them to have the same biblical vision of right and wrong. They don't have the Holy Spirit in their lives. They aren't connected to God in prayer. And, other than this verse, they probably have little knowledge of the Bible.

On the other hand, Christians do have a responsibility to point out sin in the lives of other Christians. In 1 Corinthians 5:12, Paul expresses that obligation: *"It isn't my responsibility to judge outsiders, but it certainly is your responsibility to judge those inside the church who are sinning"* (NLT).

Before you start walking around pointing out every sin by every one of your Christian friends, take a breath and consider a few other instructions.

First, there's a right way and a wrong way to view the actions of others. Don't jump to conclusions regarding some flaw you just happen to notice. John 7:24 warns, *"Stop judging by mere appearances, but instead judge correctly."*

Second, check your attitude. There should be no joy in your finger pointing. The goal is to love others to help them get back on track. *"Dear brothers and sisters, if another believer is overcome by some sin, you who are godly should gently and humbly help that person back onto the right path"* (Galatians 6:1 NLT).

Third, don't set yourself up as final judge and jury. As a matter of fact, you need to invest a lot more energy submitting yourself to God than condemning others. *"God alone, who gave the law, is the Judge. He alone has the power to save or to destroy. So what right do you have to judge your neighbor?"* (James 4:12 NLT).

Fourth, the most obvious point has already been made: *"You too will be judged."* That critical idea is confirmed in the next verse.

For in the same way you judge others, you will be judged, and with the measure you use, it will be measured to you.
—Matthew 7:2

That says it all, but keep reading the next three verses in Matthew where we find the unforgettable image of being unaware of your own sins because you have a log/beam/plank in your eye.

Why do you look at the speck of sawdust in your brother's eye and pay no attention to the plank in your own eye? How can you say to your brother, "Let me take the speck out of your eye," when all the time there is a plank in your own eye? You hypocrite, first take the plank out of your own eye, and then you will see clearly to remove the speck from your brother's eye. (Matthew 7:3–5)

When discussing sin with a fellow believer, be careful about coming off as holier-than-thou. Before you start pointing out the sins of a nonbeliever, the best advice might be "Don't do it." Instead, love them. Romans 12:9 says it well: *"Don't just pretend to love others. Really love them. Hate what is wrong. Hold tightly to what is good"* (NLT). Ever so gently, once you have developed a relationship with them, you may be able to let them know you care about how their decisions are impacting their life and the lives of those around them.

GOING DEEPER:

In the end, be careful, but don't be afraid to judge or be judged. Your words may not be well-received by nonbelievers, but the Bible requires us to bring God's truth into the light. How else are we going to be aware of false teachers as instructed in Matthew 7:15? Or help restore a brother or sister of wrongdoing as instructed in Galatians 6:1? Or expose evil deeds of those who live in darkness as described in John 3:19?

God's Word is truth. And we should never hesitate to speak truth into the lives of people we care about.
Ultimately, it should be profitable. First Peter 3:15 puts it this way: "Always be prepared to give an answer to everyone who asks you to give the reason for the hope that you have. But do this with gentleness and respect." Let's pledge to speak truth in a way that demonstrates how much we love. With gentleness and respect.

18

When I was a child, I talked like a child, I thought like a child, I reasoned like a child. When I became a man, I put the ways of childhood behind me.
—1 Corinthians 13:11

This verse (and the next) does a pretty good job of describing the seasons of cognition in the life of Christians.

There's no way a seeker or new Christian can understand and fully appreciate the complexities of the faith. The greatest theologians who ever lived spent lifetimes and wrote volumes speculating on the meaning of the Trinity, why a good God would allow suffering, how the Creator of the universe can care about each individual, and whether or not all dogs go to heaven.

Mature faith comes over several seasons. Here on earth, God's ways can never be fully understood. And even that idea is not easy to understand.

That's one of the reasons Jesus said, *"Truly I tell you, unless you change and become like little children, you will never enter the kingdom of heaven"* (Matthew 18:3). Children can't really understand the depravity of sin, the chasm between earth and heaven, the propitiatory blood of Christ, or justification by faith. But a child can certainly understand love, being naughty, feeling sorry, and finding forgiveness. All of that is a pretty good launching pad for understanding the gospel.

The second part of 1 Corinthians 13:11 presents the next season of growing up and putting away childish things. (*"When I became a man..."*) To me, that season includes a hint of sadness. Watching my own kids grow up and gently exposing them to the dark side of humanity and our world is a necessary but rueful part of parenting. Still, at some point, young people need to come to terms with the sinful nature of every individual and their need for a Savior in order to really own their faith.

Of course, that mature commitment to faith in Christ is something to celebrate on earth just as they do in heaven. Luke 15:10 says, *"There is rejoicing in the presence of the angels of God over one sinner who repents."*

Along with that mature faith comes the promise that we will one day cross the threshold to heaven, moving from death unto life. That's a promise that gives us a taste of God's glory. Yet, even as we grow in grace and knowledge, we still live in the shadows. We don't have all the answers, mostly because our human limitations couldn't handle the reality of seeing God face to face. Consider the imagery of the next verse

---

For now we see only a reflection as in a mirror;
then we shall see face to face. Now I know in part;
then I shall know fully, even as I am fully known.
—1 Corinthians 13:12

In 1 Corinthians 13:11 and the first part of verse 12, we've touched on three seasons: reasoning like a child, become a grownup, and that season when we come to understand that—like looking in a mirror—we are seeing a false reality. We don't have the tolerance or capacity to see the whole truth of who God is.

The final season of our existence comes to light in the second sentence of 1 Corinthians 13:12. All the while, God has known us fully, but we have known only partial truths. At death, crossing into eternity, we shall fully know God's glory and how His plan for us has come full circle. In other words, all those difficult theological questions you have will be answered. In an instant, all those times you asked, "Why, Lord?" will become clear.

GOING DEEPER:

Note these consecutive verses are found in 1 Corinthians 13. You may very well know this chapter as the "love chapter" of the Bible, including phrases like *"Love is patient, love is kind."* First Corinthians 13:4–8 may very well have been recited at a wedding you attended. It promises that love protects, trusts, hopes, perseveres, and never fails. The chapter ends with the idea that the greatest of all things that lasts forever is love.

So why—in the middle of all that—does the writer of 1 Corinthians include the lesson on the four seasons of understanding? Maybe because God's love (and perhaps our own ability to love) is what will help us move from childish faith to mature faith to a faith that understands human limitations and finally finding ourselves face to face with God.

Further study of 1 Corinthians 13—setting aside the romantic nature of the passage—reveals that so much of what we count on in life will ultimately pass away. Things like human knowledge and spiritual gifts will be gone (see 1 Corinthians 13:8–9). But that's okay because they were imperfect anyway. In the end, what's left is love and our perfect relationship with God.

There should be something comforting about the fact that we don't know all the answers. We can only see a dim reflection of God's plan and glory. If we ever saw a clear image of our future, it would probably blow our minds. Earlier in 1 Corinthians there is a warning that ties all of this up nicely, especially if you happen to hear someone boasting that they have it all figured out. "Anyone who claims to know all the answers doesn't really know very much. But the person who loves God is the one whom God recognizes" (1 Corinthians 8:2–3 NLT).

19

*My prayer is not that you take them out of the world but that
you protect them from the evil one.*

—John 17:15

The evening of the Last Supper begins with Jesus washing feet and ends with Jesus's longest recorded prayer in the Bible. Sometimes called "The Upper Room Discourse," Jesus prays for Himself, for His disciples, and *"for those who will believe in me through their message"* (John 17:20). For the record, He was also praying for you and me here in the 21st century.

The entire prayer—almost every word of chapter 17—feels heartfelt and unshakable. Speaking to the Father, Jesus prays His desire to bring glory to God and confirms that His own work on earth is nearly completed. Praying for His disciples, Jesus asks for God's protection and that they be sanctified by the truth. For future believers, Jesus prays for unity and that we will experience God's love and one day join Him in heaven.

John 17:15 specifically delivers a few key revelations all Christians need to appreciate and take to heart. He does not ask that we be taken *"out of the world."* We are supposed to be here, which implies we have work to do while we are here. He then asks for protection *"from the evil one,"* which indicates that Satan is actively working against us, but we can count on God to protect us.

The verse suggests that there will be a time when God will take His disciples out of the world—but not yet. The timing is not specified, except that it's probably not before their own work is complete.

For those not paying attention, Jesus then tosses out what could be a bombshell in the next verse:

They are not of the world, even as I am not of it.
—John 17:16

By this time, the disciples were well aware that Jesus was not a citizen of earth. But this might be the first time it sunk in that they also had a home in heaven. What would they do with this kind of information? What should *we* do?

First, we should admit and accept that the world is a dangerous place. It's filled with material wealth that has no eternal value and temptations to match. Pledge to heed this admonition:

> *Do not love the world or anything in the world. If anyone loves the world, love for the Father is not in them. For everything in the world—the lust of the flesh, the lust of the eyes, and the pride of life—comes not from the Father but from the world. The world and its desires pass away, but whoever does the will of God lives forever.* (1 John 2:15–17)

Note the passage begins, "*Do not love the world…*" If that caused you to pause, you're not alone. You may ask, *Why would John 3:16 say, "God so loved the world…"?* The difference is that the phrase in John 3:16 is referring to the *people* of the world, not the world itself. The earth as we know it, while beautiful as God's handiwork, is only temporary and cannot even come close to the glories of heaven. We should fully appreciate the world, but we shouldn't love it.

The second response we might have to John 17:16 is to echo Jesus's prayer that we are *in* the world, but not *of* it. Because the world is a dangerous place, many Christians believe we ought to steer clear of it and put up walls around our family to keep the world out. They harshly judge any believer who chooses to hang out with non-Christians or go to places that are popular with worldly people. Those well-meaning believers are especially vigilant when it comes to what their kids see and do.

There's a time and place for this kind of safeguarding. But what if we spent more time trusting God and praying for strength, wisdom, and courage to explore the world on His behalf? If you're a parent, while your children are under your care, there's good reason to expose them to the darkness of the world.

A story from my own life reveals the goal. Over a season, my wife and I fostered ten newborn babies. Some of them had been exposed to cocaine in the womb, which meant they were essentially recovering addicts at birth. When my teenagers saw the withdrawal tremors firsthand—sometimes even swaddling those infants nice and tight through seizures—you can imagine my own children's new realizations of how the darkness of the world needs the light of Christ. They saw the tragic consequences of drug abuse as well. Learning and understanding those truths required my kids to be exposed to the world. Yes, it's risky. But we have to intentionally establish a foothold in the world in order to reach the people who are out there in it, waiting for the love of Christ to be revealed to them.

Beyond volunteering for foster care, there are many ways to infiltrate the world and model Christ's love. Short-term mission trips. Volunteering at prisons, soup kitchens, and homeless shelters. Opening your home to international refugees. Providing diapers and baby clothes to pregnancy resource centers. It may be as simple as proactively being a lighthouse in your community and inviting new friends into your home.

GOING DEEPER:

You don't have to check your passport to confirm that your own home is not *of this world*. You just have to read Philippians 3:20–21:

> *But our citizenship is in heaven. And we eagerly await a Savior from there, the Lord Jesus Christ, who, by the power that enables him to bring everything under his control, will transform our lowly bodies so that they will be like his glorious body.*

When we are finally taken out of this world, not only do we get a new home, but we get a new body. Consider that bonus even more incentive to put yourself out there and take a few risks for the gospel.

When's the last time you got out of your comfort zone? I highly recommend trying it. But before fearlessly advancing into the world to make friends and make disciples, heed this warning from the Good Shepherd. In Matthew 10:16, Jesus said, "I am sending you out like sheep among wolves."

20

We can make our plans, but the LORD determines our steps.
—Proverbs 16:9 NLT

Here we have an agreeable proverb that is 100 percent true and makes for a nice piece of wall art. It's even a friendly statement to use when unexpected obstacles spoil your friend's perfectly reasonable plans.

Still, I would not recommend you quote Proverbs 16:9 to someone whose plans get disrupted, especially if their personal disappointment or financial loss is overwhelming. For instance, when a bride runs off with the best man, leaving the groom at the altar. Or when your brother's new million-dollar house slides into a sinkhole. Or when you set out to make the world's coolest island amusement park, but the guests are eaten by the main attraction.

In many cases, it's just not helpful to say, "Well, you know. We can make plans, but Proverbs tells us that God is going to determine the outcome." Let's all agree that we should understand and apply biblical principles when it comes to our own lives on a regular basis, but bash other people on the head with our favorite verses only occasionally.

Let's also agree that, in general, we humans should be in favor of planning. Books on leadership, parenting, finance, evangelism, construction, and so on all extol the virtues of getting organized and making plans. After all, we're supposed to draw up blueprints and do the excavation *before* laying the first brick. Proverbs 24:27 recommends, "*Do your planning and prepare your fields before building your house*" (NLT).

Who can argue with businesses and families that keep schedules and calendars? Few things get done without deadlines. A little structure and foresight make life much more pleasant. You certainly don't want to be the person who always arrives late, doesn't follow through on commitments, and shows no respect for the time and effort of others.

Thankfully, we can clarify our planning priorities simply by backtracking a few verses:

Commit your actions to the LORD,
and your plans will succeed.
—Proverbs 16:3 NLT

That good advice from Proverbs explains why sometimes God may look at your plans and direct your steps in a different direction. Perhaps you failed to first and foremost "*commit your actions to the* LORD." A little deductive reasoning will tell you that God is *less* likely to change your plans if you consult Him first.

Not surprisingly, Proverbs 16 includes quite a few more words of wisdom that apply to the ongoing challenge of making plans with the right motivation. Here are just a few.

+ "*People may be pure in their own eyes, but the* LORD *examines their motives.*" (Proverbs 16:2 NLT)

+ "*Better to have little, with godliness, than to be rich and dishonest.*" (Proverbs 16:8 NLT)

+ *"Pride goes before destruction, and haughtiness before a fall."* (Proverbs 16:18 NLT)

+ *"Those who listen to instruction will prosper; those who trust the LORD will be joyful."* (Proverbs 16:20 NLT)

GOING DEEPER:

Before moving on from Proverbs 16:3, let's consider a few reasons our plans may not succeed, even though we believe we have committed our actions to the Lord.

Did we commit our actions to the Lord, but get lazy and expect Him to do all the work? Did we start off with the best intentions, but take back control after we weren't thrilled with the early outcomes? Did we sincerely hope and pray for God to work in our lives in a way that was contrary to how He gifted us? Did He have something even better for us? Something beyond our imagination?

You may truly believe God has put something in your heart. A big dream. A project that surely would build the kingdom. And yet your well-intentioned plan doesn't succeed. How do you respond? That might be the time to go back and look again at Proverbs 16:9. This verse doesn't tell you to stop walking. It doesn't imply you failed. The verse actually encourages you to proceed with confidence. Don't give up. You can expect a new path will open up and trust that the Lord will determine your steps as promised. Just keep putting one foot in front of the other.

When your plans don't come to fruition, it could be incredibly good news. What you think is a failure is really a detour to the front door of a new friend, a rabbit trail to an unexpected adventure, or a yellow brick road that leads you home. Sure, your plan was to be at a certain place at a certain time to achieve a certain goal. But that won't always happen.

Without warning, seven other items may appear on your must-do list that are more important than your original goal. Yes, continue to make plans, but hold them loosely. Sometimes plans change simply because it's a hot summer day and Dairy Queen has two-for-one Blizzards.

21

"For my thought are not your thoughts, neither are your ways
my ways," declares the LORD.
—Isaiah 55:8

One of the central premises of this book is how Christians often have Bible verses that have personal significance. We keep them hidden in our hearts, rolling around in our brains, written on 3 x 5 cards, etched into jewelry, and embroidered and hung on our walls.

While that's a good thing, we shouldn't stop there. In many cases, we fail to pursue the deeper meaning of those verses and how to apply them to our lives and share them with others.

Isaiah 55:8 establishes that what goes on in our human minds can't possibly come close to God's omnipresence, omniscience, and omnipotence. That idea is reinforced and expanded in a doxology found in chapter 11 of Romans.

Oh, the depth of the riches of the wisdom and knowledge of God! How unsearchable his judgments, and his paths beyond tracing out! "Who has known the mind of the Lord? Or who has been his counselor?" "Who has ever given to God, that God should repay them?" For from him and through him and for him are all things. To him be the glory forever! Amen.
(Romans 11:33–36)

We take in a tremendous amount of astonishing information through our five senses. God has given us the ability to appreciate the beauty and wonder of nature. To contemplate how eagles fly, fish swim, and snakes slither. To gasp at a sunset, volcano, or canyon. To feel the warmth of a crackling campfire and the rush of a mountain stream. To experience love, anger, sadness, joy, empathy, pride, and surprise.

Yet with all those gifts and emotions, there's still no way for us to come close to fathoming the mind of the Creator. Why is that? A bit more explanation can be found in the next verse:

As the heavens are higher than the earth, so are my ways higher than your ways and my thoughts than your thoughts.
—Isaiah 55:9

God's point of view is above and beyond anything we can imagine. Our view is from earth. There's much to see and take in right here. But it's a mere sliver of creation. God shares our views, of course, but He also has a heavenly perspective.

GOING DEEPER:

For a thought-provoking object lesson of this concept, go ahead and grab that aforementioned embroidered needlepoint off your wall. If the front happens to have a clear stitching of Isaiah 55:8, it is especially relevant to this chapter, but actually any tapestry will do.

Take a moment to appreciate the beauty and composition of the top of the finished design. The design and pattern should make perfect sense. Any hand-stitched words are clearly legible. Then turn it over. The tangled zig-zag of knots and loose threads doesn't look quite so beautiful or composed. The two sides of the fabric clearly exemplify the difference between our perspective and God's.

Our messy lives often don't make sense. Our lives are filled with loose threads, zig-zags, and knots caused by times when we have lost our way, changed our minds, and stopped in our tracks. But God's heavenly perspective—one we cannot possibly share yet—reveals perfect composition. In the same way, when we're feeling massively confused, we can trust that God is still on His throne and knows what He's doing. Ultimately, there is order in the universe.

It's okay to wonder why bad things happen or how God seems to be silent or far away on occasion. He knows our heart. He also knows we can't see the bigger picture. But at the end of our lives, we will see how God's handiwork comes together and makes perfect sense. Until then, we'll have to trust the Creator to keep crafting the story of our lives. Occasionally we'll get a glimpse of His entire plan, but only if we look around and acknowledge the beauty and glory of this world He created to be our *temporary* home, until He takes us to our even more magnificent *heavenly* home.

That phrase from Isaiah 55:9, "As the heavens are higher than the earth..." may sound familiar. Here it helps us understand how God's thoughts and intentions are on a different plane than ours. Another well-known verse starts with similar words. Psalm 103:11 tells us, "For as high as the heavens are above the earth, so great is his love for those who fear him." In other words, His thoughts and His love are without limit and far beyond human imagination. Aren't you glad God is in control and not us?

22

*Therefore, go and make disciples of all the nations,
baptizing them in the name of the Father and the Son
and the Holy Spirit.*
—Matthew 28:19 NLT

The Gospel of Matthew famously ends with the Great Commission. While that phrase is not found in Scripture, Jesus's words are a clear command to enthusiastically tell others what He did on the cross and what He has done in our own lives.

Many—perhaps most—Christians reference this verse, emphasizing the words *"make disciples of all the nations"* as they pertain to the global outreach done by missionaries. That's a valid perspective. Quite a few mission organizations validate that idea by incorporating some or all of Matthew 28:19 in their logos along with graphic images of globes and maps.

Their ambitions are inspiring and worthy of our applause. But we shouldn't settle for merely cheering them on from the sidelines. The Great Commission isn't just for Christians who get on airplanes and cross international borders. Your own family members, neighbors, and everyone you meet also need Christ. Even if you give generously to World Relief, TEAM, or Bible League International, you still have a personal part to play in the way Matthew ends his gospel. Especially when you consider the next verse:

Teach these new disciples to obey all the commands
I have given you. And be sure of this:
I am with you always, even to the end of the age.
—Matthew 28:20 NLT

In one sense, disciples are made in a moment. When an individual—your neighbor or a stranger living on the other side of the planet—realizes their sinful condition and accepts the free gift of grace, they have found salvation. They are born again. Their sins are washed clean. They have crossed the line from death unto eternal life, and the door is open to all kinds of wonderful gifts and opportunities.

But most followers of Christ agree that a one-time decision is just the beginning of discipleship. A new believer has to walk through that door and begin to *"obey all the commands"* given by Jesus. There's work that needs to be done. There's only one way the Great Commission can be fulfilled and that's when believers—new and longtime followers—commit to the steps laid out in the last two verses of Matthew.

These verses lay out a three-part plan. First, baptism is the initial outward sign of our inward washing. Then, the commands of Scripture—found in all 66 books of the Bible—need to be understood, taught, and obeyed. Following the Word as a way of life brings purpose and joy to this life and the next. Third, it's all possible because Jesus promises to be with us always through the presence of the Holy Spirit.

That's how to make disciples…who make other disciples. Again, this assignment is not limited to pastors, missionaries, and theology professors. It's an expectation and privilege for every Christian.

GOING DEEPER:

More than just a response to the Great Commission, there are many other motivations for evangelism. Your identity as a believer requires it. Once we have accepted God's free gift of grace, He speaks through us:

> *We are therefore Christ's ambassadors, as though God were making his appeal through us.* (2 Corinthians 5:20)

In addition, there are many in heaven rooting for us. Legions of saints and angels are tracking our efforts and cheering us to lead others to repentance and faith.

> *Therefore, since we are surrounded by such a great cloud of witnesses, let us throw off everything that hinders and the sin that so easily entangles. And let us run with perseverance the race marked out for us.* (Hebrews 12:1)

> *In the same way, I tell you, there is rejoicing in the presence of the angels of God over one sinner who repents.* (Luke 15:10)

Finally, it's personally rewarding. You'll experience joy alongside anyone you lead to Christ.

> *The harvesters are paid good wages, and the fruit they harvest is people brought to eternal life. What joy awaits both the planter and the harvester alike!* (John 4:36 NLT)

You might think—since these would be His final words to His disciples—Jesus should have re-emphasized the two greatest commandments as set forth in Matthew 22:37, 39: "*Love the Lord your God with all your heart and with all your soul and with all your mind.*" And "*Love your neighbor as yourself.*"

With the Great Commission, that's exactly what He did.

One other takeaway from Matthew 28:19 is often overlooked. This verse is one of the few places in the Bible that specifically names all three members of the Trinity— "the Father and...the Son and...the Holy Spirit."

23

Pray without ceasing.
—1 Thessalonians 5:17 NASB

Take note: This three-word verse is not a recommendation. It is an imperative statement. You could even consider it a requirement for those who follow Christ. But how—you may ask—is it possible for any individual to pray continually?

To be clear, the instruction does not say, "Kneel nonstop" or "Close your eyes and fold your hands around the clock." Nor does it instruct us to "live in a church" or "mumble memorized prayers hour after hour."

It turns out, prayer is not about the bombastic use of lots of fancy words. Matthew 6:7 confirms, *"When you pray, do not keep on babbling like pagans, for they think they will be heard because of their many words."*

It's also not for show. Matthew 6:5 warns, *"When you pray, do not be like the hypocrites, for they love to pray standing in the synagogues and on the street corners to be seen by others. Truly I tell you, they have received their reward in full."*

Prayer is about being in communion with Jesus. *"God is faithful, who has called you into fellowship with his Son, Jesus Christ our Lord"* (1 Corinthians 1:9).

After inviting Him into your life, your prayers should be all about striving to join your heart with His, unifying your mind with His, matching your ambition, desire, and dreams with His. It's about surrendering to the Spirit and to His truth and grace as a fountain that overflows from our inmost soul.

To pray without ceasing requires us to live under the reality of Galatians 2:20. *"I have been crucified with Christ and I no longer live, but Christ lives in me. The life I now live in the body, I live by faith in the Son of God, who loved me and gave himself for me."*

With that kind of empowerment, it makes me wonder what else I can do! Let's take a peek at the three words—*"pray without ceasing"*—framed by the surrounding verses:

Rejoice always, pray without ceasing, in everything give thanks; for this is the will of God for you in Christ Jesus.
—1 Thessalonians 5:16–18 NASB

Those three succinct imperative statements deserve to be unpacked. *"Rejoice always." "Pray without ceasing." "In everything give thanks."*

To rejoice always requires us to find joy in both good times and bad. We may not always be happy, but the hope we have in Christ gives us a patience and strength that allows us to experience the ongoing deep joy that is so elusive to those who do not know the Savior.

To pray without ceasing requires us to understand that prayer is even more than adoration, contrition, thanksgiving, and supplication. As expressed above, it's adopting the mind of Christ.

To give thanks in everything requires us to trust that in the end all things work together for good. This includes our good and the good of our community and the world, as discussed in a previous chapter, in God's timing.

Committing to those three imperatives should leave us feeling confident because the passage ends with *"this is the will of God for you in Christ Jesus."*

GOING DEEPER:

Of course, theologians and pastors have been preaching and writing on the topic of prayer for thousands of years. I'm not sure who came up with it, but one popular "formula" for prayer is A-C-T-S: adoration, confession, thanksgiving, and supplication. I've heard the suggestion that we should employ that acronym to begin our prayer time with praise, move into asking forgiveness, express gratitude, and then end with humble requests to God.

Not to debate any of the scholars who suggest the four-step formula, but that concept seems to disregard the idea of our ability to *"pray without ceasing."*

Since we are in unceasing fellowship with Christ, the communication would be ongoing without beginning or end. We are constantly in worship, being broken about our sins, living in gratitude, and turning to God and recognizing Him as our sole provider. We're not doing one after another; it's all happening simultaneously.

There's an interesting consequence when we are aware of God in the midst of every thought and action. Our sins become much more obvious! Going about our lives in constant prayer does not guarantee that we won't sin. We still have the choice to ignore God's guidance. But we know it when we do!

You might say there are benefits as well as drawbacks when we *"pray without ceasing."* God's disappointment and God's approval will always be at the top of your mind.

Congratulations. As an authentic believer, you are already a master multitasker. Every second of every day, you are equipped to pray, rejoice, and give thanks. But don't stop there. There are scores of other imperative statements in the Bible. Actions to take. Words to say. Strangers to love. Enemies to forgive. By abiding in the three prompts from 1 Thessalonians 5:16–18—prayer, joy, gratitude—you'll be a very attractive witness of how God works in the lives of believers.

24

Finally, brothers and sisters, whatever is true, whatever is noble, whatever is right, whatever is pure, whatever is lovely, whatever is admirable—if anything is excellent or praiseworthy—think about such things.
—Philippians 4:8

Have you noticed that a vast array of today's so-called "entertainment" is violent, depressing, graphic, filthy, angry, and devoid of hope? Even worse than the obvious assault on our senses may be the subtle systematic perversion of our worldview. In the name of tolerance or progress, any creative or personal choice made by anyone at any time is not to be judged.

Frankly, we shouldn't be surprised. Protecting values is not the primary responsibility of most film studios, network executives, publishers, or music producers. Morality is not in their job description. Their explicit assignment is to make as much money as possible for their companies. If they don't believe in God, why would they follow a biblical worldview when pushing their products to the marketplace?

If it's not the fault of those who generate the depressing, soul-crushing books, movies, art, and music, whose fault is it? Well, perhaps, it is yours and mine. If we're honest with ourselves, we're the ones *allowing* it to happen. We're not taking a stand with our families, friends, neighbors, and colleagues. Even worse, sometimes we're actually supporting it with our viewing, reading, and listening. When we contribute to the profits, we are actually sending a message that such content is welcome!

If you're feeling a bit convicted by this idea, will you join me in committing to follow the guidance of Philippians 4:8? Let's be intentional about setting our mind on things that are excellent and praiseworthy. That's the first logical step in our biblical response. Romans 12:2 tells us that knowing God's pleasing and perfect will begins with turning our mind away from worldly ways. *"Do not conform to the pattern of this world, but be transformed by the renewing of your mind. Then you will be able to test and approve what God's will is—his good, pleasing and perfect will."*

Getting our own mind right is step one. Step two is described in the next verse:

Whatever you have learned or received or heard from me,
or seen in me—put it into practice.
And the God of peace will be with you.
—Philippians 4:9

After we commit to filling our own heads with good stuff, then we need to act outwardly. We need to put into practice the uplifting and encouraging things we learn, receive, hear, read, text, and post. This means doing more than just sharing and retweeting nice thoughts. This means doing nice things for others.

There's a direct connection between what you receive and what you give. Garbage in/garbage out, right? The first time they watch an R-rated film with blood splashing everywhere or unmarried couples hooking up without consequence, a high percentage of viewers feel dirty, like they need to take a shower. As they continue to view content like this, they become desensitized. The once-unacceptable behavior is normalized. Even so, what they are taking in continues to affect them. They may not even realize it, but that process of self-degradation has an impact. Suddenly they are less likely to pick flowers for grandma, make a casserole for a shut-in neighbor, or write a thank-you note to the high school teacher who had a positive impact on their life.

What books, movies, art, and music are you taking in? Do those things more often affect you negatively or inspire you to do things you're proud of? Do the books you read leave you with hope worth sharing? Do the songs you listen to inspire you to love more and be your best self? Is God honored by your choices and the actions inspired by those choices? You don't have to exclusively read books from Christian publishers, watch films by Christian production houses, and listen to music from Christian artists. But if you've found yourself drifting away from positive influences, those are obvious places to turn. Those who produce inspirational or Christian art and media need your support, and by "voting with our dollars," we show that positive entertainment is worth producing.

GOING DEEPER:

Technology might be forcing your hand when it comes to your entertainment choices. You're at a crossroads, and you need to make a decision. You are probably aware that tracking software and preference analysis has created an algorithm just for you. It guesses what you want and sends you more of it. That means your clicks and viewing choices today determine what you will be offered tomorrow. If there's more and more crud coming your way, there's a good chance you invited it.

Maybe this is all good news. Big tech and profit-driven entertainment will continue their attempt to lure you into their dark view of the world. But the way technology tracks our individual lives, we can now actually help determine what comes into our own home.

> **Choose your personal input wisely. Paraphrasing Philippians 4:8-9: If you want to live in peace, you know what to do. Fill your mind and heart with the beautiful and wondrous elements of God's creation. This will inspire your work and play, and God's peace will find you and fill you.**

25

My Father, if it is possible, may this cup be taken from me.
Yet not as I will, but as you will.
—Matthew 26:39

Once you realize what really happened in the garden of Gethsemane late on that Thursday night, you can never forget it.

Jesus had come to a point of no return. Since the beginning of time, His destiny was determined. Scores of prophecies in the Hebrew Bible had predicted the place He would be born, the life He would live, and the way He would die.

We know the story well. The moment Jesus—and all of humanity—gained victory over death culminated at Golgotha. Images of the crucifix hanging on the walls of churches and on gold chains commemorate the history-changing event. But it doesn't happen without the events and the incomparable prayer on the Mount of Olives. Matthew 26:36–39 sets the scene:

> *Then Jesus went with his disciples to a place called Gethsemane, and he said to them, "Sit here while I go over there and pray." He took Peter and the two sons of Zebedee along with him, and he began to be sorrowful and troubled. Then he said to them, "My soul is overwhelmed with sorrow to the point of death. Stay here and keep watch with me." Going a little farther, he fell with his face to the ground and prayed, "My*

Father, if it is possible, may this cup be taken from me. Yet not as I will, but as you will."

There in the garden of Gethsemane, and in fact during His entire life, Jesus had the ability to see into the future. His knowledge of what would happen includes all of eternity and the horrific events that would take place the very next day. But what exactly was *"this cup"* that caused Jesus to make this appeal?

As the Son of God, He knew His mission. But as a human, He undoubtedly felt fear of the physical suffering and death He would soon face. Moreover, the idea of bearing the weight of all the sin of the world—past, present, and future—would have been overwhelming. The enormous dark abyss of sin, Jesus knew, would also separate Him from the Father as the culmination of His mortality became real. In that instant, what happens to the Trinity? For that moment—saturated with sin—did Jesus fall out of favor with God? That's a question too big to wrestle with here.

In the midst of this supernatural turn of events, which we cannot begin to comprehend, comes a lesson we can use in our own human lives. You'll see it instantly when you read the next verse:

Then he returned to his disciples and found them sleeping. "Couldn't you men keep watch with me for one hour?" he asked Peter. "Watch and pray so that you will not fall into temptation. The spirit is willing, but the flesh is weak."
—Matthew 26:40

The juxtaposition of these consecutive verses is staggering. At one moment, Jesus is surrendering His will to the Creator of the universe in anticipation of the most important event in history. The very next verse has Him confronting His best friends about how they have disappointed Him.

This betrayal occurs on top of all the other events in the garden. Collectively, the Gospel accounts include the appearance of an angel to strengthen Jesus, His sweat falling like drops of blood to the ground, a parade of torches, a kiss of betrayal, a slashing sword, a miraculous healing, and the disciples fleeing the scene. (See Matthew 26:36–56 and Luke 22:39–52.)

In many ways, this was Jesus's moment of truth. In the midst of the turmoil, it turns out His human sensibilities left Him looking for a way out. Physically, His body was breaking down. The religious leaders were hunting Him. One disciple had sold Him out for 30 pieces of silver. And while Jesus appealed in desperation to God, His best friends declined to pray and chose to nap.

GOING DEEPER:

Looking back, what a gift Jesus's pain and desire not to suffer is to Christians today. No matter what you and I might be going through, Jesus understands. We can respond to our most harrowing moments of truth the same way He did. Jesus took His honest heartfelt appeal to God and gained the grace He needed.

> *For we do not have a high priest who is unable to empathize with our weaknesses, but we have one who has been tempted in every way, just as we are—yet he did not sin. Let us then approach God's throne of grace with confidence, so that we may receive mercy and find grace to help us in our time of need.* (Hebrews 4:15–16)

You may not be sweating blood. You may not have soldiers with torches tracking you down. You may not have all the weight of the world on your shoulders. But when you've hit bottom, know that you can confidently do what Jesus did: take it all to God.

The prayer at Gethsemane was a moment in time that could have left the human race unmistakably godforsaken. Jesus prayed. God answered. Essentially God was telling His Son, "No." Yet somehow, it all worked out for good.

The garden of Gethsemane teaches us that good friends can disappoint you. They'll fall asleep or scatter like the wind when you need them most. They may even deny they know you. When that happens, consider it another chance to extend grace. After all, you may need your friends to do the same for you someday.

26

Trust in the Lord *with all your heart and lean not on your
own understanding; in all your ways submit to him,
and he will make your paths straight.*
—Proverbs 3:5–6

This is a great passage that leads to a reasonable follow-up question: What happens when we don't trust and don't submit to the Lord? What if we attempt to tackle a problem without Him by leaning on our own human understanding?

Well, maybe it works out fine. It's possible our gut instinct gets it right. I'm actually a fan of common sense. We humans have all kinds of effective decision-making strategies in our God-given brains. In some cases, we can phone a friend or ask for help from the audience. As intelligent beings, we can examine history and know what worked last time. Trusting the experts—doctors, physicists, scientists—is a tried-and-true tactic in today's educated world.

But sometimes science gets it wrong. As the experts gain more information, new theories emerge. Minds change. Conventional wisdom is proven wrong. Examples are many:

When Pluto was discovered in 1930, it was deemed the ninth planet in our solar system. In 2006, poor Pluto was reclassified as a dwarf planet.

For decades, doctors prescribed milk for treating ulcers, believing it coated the stomach and relieved symptoms. In the 1980s, they discovered milk stimulates the production of stomach acid, thereby aggravating the condition.

For fifteen hundred years, scientists recognized Aristotle's idea of spontaneous generation, asserting that maggots, fleas, tapeworms, and other lower creatures sprang to life out of inanimate matter or dead flesh. In the mid-19th century, Louis Pasteur proved the idea was nonsense.

Also, scientists are now mostly in agreement that the earth is not the center of the universe, toads don't give you warts, Y2K did not send humanity back to the stone age, and an apple a day is not a foolproof way to keep doctors away.

To be sure, biology, chemistry, physics, agronomy, archaeology, astronomy, genetics, meteorology, and just about every branch of science have done great things for mankind. The concept of science should not be dismissed or mocked. But never should it take precedent over trusting, respecting, and fearing the Lord. Further enlightenment comes to light in the next two verses:

Do not be wise in your own eyes; fear the Lord *and shun evil. This will bring health to your body and nourishment to your bones.*
—Proverbs 3:7–8

This passage reiterates the warning not to trust your own eyes and to be in awe of the Lord. But then it gives some critical additional instruction: *"Shun evil."* This suggests that leaning first and foremost on our own human understanding opens the door to Satan, a mistake that will surely make your paths crooked.

Furthermore, there's a direct benefit to trusting, respecting, and fearing the Lord. Your health depends on it. Because we can put some trust in science, it's a good idea to head to a hospital when you're sick, but I hope you agree that having God on your side is better in the long run than being treated by the finest doctors in the world. By the way, it was God who gave your doctors the desire and the ability to practice medicine.

GOING DEEPER:

This entire passage from Proverbs 3 brings to mind a range of ideas that came to light during the COVID-19 crisis. Trusting God. The limitations of human understanding. Trusting science. Shunning evil. And the propensity for humans to think we are smarter than we really are. The debate left the Christian community fiercely divided. Too many well-intentioned believers began to think they were wise in their own eyes. Looking back, a little more humility and fear of the Lord may have served us all well.

Humans made in the image of God have been given the ability to create, imagine, invent, heal, breed livestock, plant seeds, and reap many a harvest. Equipped by the Creator, there is much we can achieve on our own. The problem comes when we look back on a successful season of life and take too much pride in our work. By leaning on our own human understanding and instincts, we bask in the glory of having achieved great things in the eyes of the world. But consider this: even if we seem to have gotten it exactly right, God may have had something even better in mind if only we had fully trusted and submitted to Him.

27

Cast your bread upon the waters,
for you will find it after many days.
—Ecclesiastes 11:1 ESV

Close your eyes and you can almost hear the homespun delivery of an old-time country pastor saying, "Cast your bread on the water…" But what does it mean?

Let's eliminate a few possibilities. That preacher and Solomon (the writer of Ecclesiastes) are not suggesting we should toss our ciabatta, pita, or sourdough into a pond. No one likes soggy bread (except maybe ducks!).

Some have interpreted this verse literally, as a recommendation to ship baked goods to other countries and profit from maritime trade. However, financial profit is really not a theme found in Ecclesiastes. As a matter of fact, gaining wealth is one of several pursuits Solomon describes as "meaningless."

It's possible that the recommendation to *"cast your bread"* is telling us that being generous to the poor will result in some kind of reward. That idea is confirmed in the New Testament: *"Give, and it will be given to you. A good measure, pressed down, shaken together and running over, will be poured into your lap. For with the measure you use, it will be measured to you"* (Luke 6:38).

Just to be clear, when you give to charity, you shouldn't expect a *financial* kickback, but you can expect some fresh joy or blessing.

Most certainly, you can't buy your way into heaven. But in the case of the rich young ruler, Jesus told him to *"sell your possessions and give to the poor, and you will have treasure in heaven"* (Matthew 19:21). Based on that example, there is a probable connection between casting your bread generously to those in need and having an authentic faith that gains eternal life.

I hope you are not offended by a paraphrase offered by 19th-century novelist Louisa May Alcott, author of *Little Women*, who purportedly wrote, "Cast your bread upon the waters, and after many days it will come back buttered." That amusing restatement hits upon the idea that while the outcome is not certain, there's a good chance you will be surprised and delighted when you give, invest, risk, or devote yourself to a worthy cause.

So what does it mean to cast our bread upon water, and what will we find after many days? Skipping down a few lines in your Bible we find the clarifying verse:

In the morning sow your seed, and at evening withhold not your hand, for you do not know which will prosper, this or that, or whether both alike will be good.
—Ecclesiastes 11:6 ESV

To be clear, this verse does not contradict the much-quoted verse, *"A man reaps what he sows"* (Galatians 6:7). Instead, it speaks to the unpredictability of all our human efforts and the uncertain results of any sowing and reaping we might do.

We can choose to work and invest here and now (in the morning). We can also choose to work and invest later (in the evening). But actually, we should do both, because we can't be sure if either or both of our sowing seasons will come to fruition. Covering our bases guarantees a reward—perhaps double our expectations!

In other words, keep hustling. Seize every opportunity. Sow day and night. As we know, healthy seed can fall on rocky soil, a dry path, among weeds, or in good soil. (See Matthew 13:1–9, 18–23). As sowers, we just don't know when and where fresh-tilled soil awaits or the wheat will find root, so that at the harvest the grain can be ground and the flour can be made into bread.

GOING DEEPER:

All of this discussion brings us full circle to what the bread is and where we are meant to be casting it.

I believe Solomon is most likely predicting the coming Messiah—Jesus, the Bread of Life—and the water represents the sea of people eager for purpose and hope. Ephesians 11:1, 6 is reminding us to be ready to share the good news with anyone at any time, morning or evening. If we sow the truth of what Jesus has done in our life, then we can reasonably expect a harvest.

We may not know the result of casting our bread upon the water for days or years. But it will return, maybe even buttered. Or toasted! Or swabbed with homemade jam! What's more, we can take great joy in being part of the harvest and knowing that we have been part of a plan that promises that those who accept the Bread of Life will never be hungry or thirsty again. *"I am the bread of life. Whoever comes to me will never go hungry, and whoever believes in me will never be thirsty"* (John 6:35).

> We have to be careful about any action that leads us to expect an immediate return. God doesn't work that way. Put a buck in the basket and He doesn't promise a financial return. Share the gospel with your work colleague and he may not come to Christ. Bend over to tie the shoelaces of a small child and they may kick you in the shin. But that's all okay. There's authentic joy simply in glorifying God. It may be undisclosed for quite a while, but the Bible also promises, "The one who sows righteousness reaps a sure reward" (Proverbs 11:18).

28

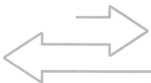

Teacher, don't you care if we drown?
—Mark 4:38

You've probably imagined the scene when the disciples, recently chosen by Jesus, find themselves in a squall on the Sea of Galilee. This should be no big deal to a group of seasoned fishermen, right? Still, terrified of being capsized, the new recruits wake Jesus, who was in the stern enjoying a well-deserved nap.

You may recall that Jesus had just spent much of the day delivering parables to thousands of listeners gathered on the shoreline, and then He had to explain the meaning of His words to His slow-on-the-uptake disciples. Mark 4:39 reports that after being so rudely awaken, Jesus efficiently calms the storm. Then, rather than chastising the disciples, He asks them two questions in the next verse:

Why are you so afraid? Do you still have no faith?
—Mark 4:40

By answering a question with a question, Jesus prompts the disciples to reflect on what they have already seen and heard. Apparently the men still had much to learn because, according to Mark 4:41,

"They were terrified and asked each other, 'Who is this? Even the wind and the waves obey him!'"

The Bible documents at least 25 times when Jesus responded to a question with a question. Jesus's model of communication turns out to be an excellent strategy for many of life's conundrums. Looking at a few more occasions can provide further insight into His character and provide a strategy anyone can use when dealing with conflict, delivering a lesson, or having their faith challenged.

In Matthew 15:33–34, the disciples ask Jesus, *"Where could we get enough bread in this remote place to feed such a crowd?"* Jesus asks a question that helps identify the resources at hand: *"How many loaves do you have?"*

In Luke 2:48–49, Mary and Joseph finally track down their 12-year-old son who had been left behind in Jerusalem. He had been lost for three days, but when they find young Jesus in the temple courts engaging with the religious teachers, He doesn't seem the least upset or apologetic. His mother asks, *"Son, why have you treated us like this? Your father and I have been anxiously searching for you"* (v. 48). Sounding like a typical preteen, Jesus asks, *"Why were you searching for me?...Didn't you know I had to be in my Father's house?"* (v. 49).

In Luke 10:25–37, after Jesus teaches about loving your neighbor, a lawyer asks, *"Who is my neighbor?"* (v. 29). Jesus responds by telling the parable known as "The Good Samaritan." Then He asks, *"Which of these three do you think was a neighbor to the man who fell into the hands of robbers?"* (v. 36). That question hit home especially because there was deep hatred between the Jews and the Samaritans.

In John 13:37, Peter asks, *"Lord, why can't I follow you now? I will lay down my life for you."* Knowing that Peter will soon deny Him three times, Jesus asks the loaded question, *"Will you really lay down your life for me?"* (v. 38).

Over and over, Jesus models the art of asking questions. It's a beneficial strategy for any believer who sees the value in sharing their faith with love and respect, rather than a bullhorn and a club.

In conflict, in debate, or simply trying to show how much you really care about another person, consider taking a moment to ask a clarifying question. It gives both parties a chance to determine what they really want and how much they are willing to risk. In many cases, the initial question may turn out to be unanswerable. In other cases, the answer will become crystal clear.

GOING DEEPER:

Perhaps the most infamous scene in which Jesus clarifies a major point of contention for ancient times as well as today's world occurs in Mark 12:13–17. The religious leaders were determined to take down the troublemaker who threatened their power and revenue stream.

> *Later they sent some of the Pharisees and Herodians to Jesus to catch him in his words. They came to him and said, "Teacher, we know that you are a man of integrity. You aren't swayed by others, because you pay no attention to who they are; but you teach the way of God in accordance with the truth. Is it right to pay the imperial tax to Caesar or not? Should we pay or shouldn't we?" But Jesus knew their hypocrisy. "Why are you trying to trap me?" he asked. "Bring me a denarius and let me look at it." They brought the coin, and he asked them, "Whose portrait is this? And whose inscription?" "Caesar's," they replied. Then Jesus said to them, "Give back to Caesar what is Caesar's and to God what is God's." And they were amazed at him.*

Next time you're paging through the Gospels, take note of Jesus's questions. He asks more than a hundred of them. I recommend that everyone own a red-letter edition of the Bible to easily identify these passages. Having the words of Jesus in red under-scores His teachings and, in many cases, offers the exact words you can use to tell others about Him.

Is God calling you to do more one-on-one evangelism? Do you have friends and colleagues who need Jesus? It can be a challenge. Sometimes you don't know what to say.

You certainly don't want to be the guy who comes off as holier-than-thou and pretends to have all the answers.

Well, good news. You don't have all the answers, but you do have the ability to ask questions. Asking sincere questions of people in your life shows that you care. With that in mind, in your next conversation with someone to whom God has called you to minister, do less telling and more asking.

29

*Love the LORD your God with all your heart and with all
your soul and with all your strength.*
—Deuteronomy 6:5

For context, Deuteronomy is the last book of the Pentateuch, the
first five books of the Bible, and includes the final public addresses
by Moses to the nation of Israel.

Moses first presented the Ten Commandments almost 40
years earlier at the base of Mount Sinai, described in Exodus 20.
In Deuteronomy 5, Moses again articulates the Decalogue and
then describes how he saw the glory of God, heard the voice of
God, and received the two stone tablets.

In that same oratory, Moses calls upon the Israelites to follow
these laws, fear the Lord, and walk in such a way that they will live
and prosper. Then in Deuteronomy 6:5, he delivers what may be
considered a surprising summary of the law. His words, *"Love the
LORD your God with all your heart and with all your soul and with
all your strength,"* not only encapsulate the entire law, but they also
foreshadow the words of Jesus in Matthew 22:37.

Because Moses knows the importance of passing on a legacy
of faith, he gives specific instructions—especially to parents—
regarding best practices for how and when to talk about the law in
the very next verses:

These commandments that I give you today are to be on your
hearts. Impress them on your children.
Talk about them when you sit at home and when you walk
along the road, when you lie down and when you get up.
Tie them as symbols on your hands and bind them on your
foreheads. Write them on the doorframes of your houses
and on your gates.
—Deuteronomy 6:6–9

With these words, Moses delivers one of the best ways to *"love the*
Lord your God with all your heart and with all your soul and with all
your strength," which is to pass your faith on to your children. He
wisely points out that this requires more than a one-time speech.
It's about building relationships. Handing down spiritual truths is
a way of life.

Parents, as you apply this passage in today's culture, may I suggest talking to your kids about stuff that matters during TV commercials, while riding in the car, strolling down the road, or tucking them in at night, or over breakfast with heart-shaped waffles.

In addition to sharing your faith through your loving relationship with your family, feel free to display posters, needlepoint, and plaques with favorite verses of Scripture on the walls of your home. Even bracelets, wristbands, necklaces, and T-shirts could be ways to express your faith. For some, a tasteful tattoo of your life verse on your forearm may be the 21st-century way to *"tie them as*
symbols on your hands" and tell current and future generations of your commitment to God's promises.

GOING DEEPER:

The entire book of Deuteronomy is Moses's final loving
instructions to Israel, reminding them of who God is and what He

has done. Other quotable passages express why His laws are worth following and passing on.

> *Know therefore that the* LORD *your God is God; he is the faithful God, keeping his covenant of love to a thousand generations of those who love him and keep his commandments.*
>
> (Deuteronomy 7:9)

Moses definitely wasn't perfect, and he helped the people of Israel repent and learn through many of their own mistakes. In the end, only two individuals who began the journey from Egypt would enter the promised land: Joshua and Caleb. The failures of an entire generation kept them from abundant life here on earth. Still, God was faithful to the nation and future generations.

Following the instructions of Moses, be intentional about writing the words of the law on your heart and in your home. Impress them on your children. The law is valuable for guidance and revealing our sins. Thankfully, like the nation of Israel, we can count on God's love, patience, and faithfulness, even when we mess up.

Parents, the way to share your faith with your children is to enter their world and invite them to enter yours.
Consider for a moment the world your son or daughter has created. Their bedroom, their circle of friends, their teams and clubs, their safe zone, their aura. Where and how can you earn the right to be part of that world? On the flip side, make sure your children know who you really are and what's important to you. Then find a way for those kids you love so much to join in your work, hobby, and life passions. That will earn you the right to share from your own heart the truths that really matter.

30

Do not be afraid.
—Matthew 28:5

Scores of times throughout the Bible, when an angel appears to a mere mortal, one of the very first things the angel says is some version of, "Fear not." That shouldn't come as a surprise.

Typically, angels appear to just one person, who is probably scared out of his or her sandals. Often the angel's message is unexpected and life-changing. Plus, they're angels! Whether it's a cherubim, seraphim, or some other classification, the appearance of these heavenly messengers will surely induce jaw-dropping confusion and wonder.

Not every angelic appearance in the Bible is expressed in detail, but each visit was surely unforgettable. The angels described in Ezekiel had an overall human form but had four wings and four faces—a human, lion, ox, and eagle—looked like burning torches, and had lightning shooting back and forth between them. (See Ezekiel 1:5–18.)

The angels that show up before and right after the birth of Jesus all were polite enough to say, "Don't be afraid," when they dropped in on at least four occasions.

When Zechariah saw him, he was startled and was gripped with fear. But the angel said to him: "Do not be afraid,

Zechariah; your prayer has been heard. Your wife Elizabeth will bear you a son, and you are to call him John."

(Luke 1:11–13)

The angel said to her, "Do not be afraid, Mary; you have found favor with God. You will conceive and give birth to a son, and you are to call him Jesus."   (Luke 1:30–31)

An angel of the Lord appeared to him in a dream and said, "Joseph son of David, do not be afraid to take Mary home as your wife, because what is conceived in her is from the Holy Spirit."   (Matthew 1:20)

There were shepherds living out in the fields nearby, keeping watch over their flocks at night. An angel of the Lord appeared to them, and the glory of the Lord shone around them, and they were terrified. But the angel said to them, "Do not be afraid. I bring you good news that will cause great joy for all the people."   (Luke 2:8–10)

After all four angelic instructions to have no fear, did you notice the next verses? They all delivered welcome albeit startling news. The angel Gabriel told Zechariah his prayers had been answered. Later, the same angel Gabriel told the virgin girl, Mary, that she had found favor with God and was impossibly pregnant. Joseph was given specific instructions and news that kept him from quietly divorcing Mary. The shepherds were told the universally joyful news that a Savior had been born.

Some 33 years later, another angel appeared with even more amazing news. At dawn on the third day after Jesus's crucifixion, Mary Magdalene and another woman went to the tomb. After an earthquake, they arrived to see an angel, whose appearance was *"like lightning,"* wearing clothes as *"white as snow"* (Matthew 28:3). He was sitting on the stone that he had just rolled away from the entrance to the tomb. The guards that had been posted were so scared they couldn't move. The angel said to the two women, "*Do not be afraid*" (v. 5). Then the angel delivered the greatest message in the history of the world in the next verse:

I know that you are looking for Jesus, who was crucified.
He is not here; he has risen, just as he said.
Come and see the place where he lay.
—Matthew 28:5–6

Moments later, as instructed by the angel, the women raced from the scene to tell the disciples the stunning news. On the way, they suddenly met the risen Christ, who also said, "*Do not be afraid*" (v. 10). To be clear, Jesus was not an angel, ghost, or hallucination, and was very much alive.

Over the next 40 days, Jesus would teach His disciples and prepare them for the task of telling His story. He appeared to many, proving beyond doubt that He had been raised from the dead by the power of God. Later, the apostle Paul would write that "*he appeared to more than five hundred of the brothers and sisters at the same time, most of whom are still living*" (1 Corinthians 15:6).

GOING DEEPER:

You don't have to believe all the stories you hear of angels. But you should believe some of them. Angels are referenced more than 200 times in the Bible. Hebrews 13:2 confirms the reality of angels at work today: "*Do not forget to show hospitality to strangers, for by so doing some people have shown hospitality to angels without knowing it.*"

Open your heart and mind to the possibility that angels (as well as fallen angels or demons) are at work every day in the lives of people around the world. Admit they have more power than you and I. But, to borrow a phrase, *"Do not be afraid, "* because you can call on the name of Jesus, who has power over all.

When you hear stories of angels rescuing a girl from a burning car or holding a patient's hand overnight in the hospital, it's okay to be skeptical. But also don't be surprised. Some church traditions may place too much emphasis on angels, but there is enough evidence and testimony to affirm that angels are showing up and working miracles every day.

31

I am the good shepherd.
The good shepherd lays down his life for the sheep.
—John 10:11

We love the image of the Good Shepherd. Generations of Sunday-school children have adored flannelgraphs with fluffy felt sheep and a smiling shepherd. Even adults find comfort in the gentle shepherd who shows up in Psalm 23, leading us beside still waters and protecting us through the darkest valley.

We are thrilled that He calls us by name. We recognize His voice. He cares about even one lost sheep, which we know could be someone we love desperately who has made destructive choices. Best of all, we have the promise in John 10:15 from the Good Shepherd that *"I lay down my life for the sheep."*

The image of us as sheep and God as shepherd is sprinkled throughout the Bible. The prophet Ezekiel describes the difference between a good shepherd and a bad shepherd when he foretells the coming of Messiah. (See Ezekiel 34:1–24.) Psalm 100:3 exclaims with joy, *"Know that the LORD is God. It is he who made us, and we are his; we are his people, the sheep of his pasture."*

Right before Jesus identifies Himself as *"the good shepherd,"* He underscores the most important reason shepherds need to be vigilant and devoted to the task. You may recognize the previous verse:

*The thief comes only to steal and kill and destroy; I have
come that they may have life, and have it to the full.*
—John 10:10

What a contrast! This verse clearly lays out the choice we have. We can follow Satan for death and destruction or stay close to the Good Shepherd for an abundant life—a life He purchased when He lay down His life for ours.

A closer look at John 10:1–18 actually reveals several warnings for those who identify with the sheep. Jesus, who identifies Himself as the sheepgate, warns that any man who does not enter by the gate is a thief and robber. Jesus also confirms that thieves and robbers may come after sheep, but the sheep will not respond to their voice. That's because the more time you spend with Jesus, the more discerning you will be when it comes to the voices in your life.

An adjacent passage introduces another aspect of the sheep/ shepherd relationship. Apparently, a hired hand is sometimes employed to look after sheep. But can he be trusted?

*The hired hand is not the shepherd and does not own the
sheep. So when he sees the wolf coming, he abandons the sheep
and runs away. Then the wolf attacks the flock and scatters
it. The man runs away because he is a hired hand and cares
nothing for the sheep.*   (John 10:12–13)

Let's take a closer look at this cast of characters. The Good Shepherd is constant and attentive. The thief and the wolf are undeniable threats and clearly have ill intent. The wolf's fur and fangs are dead giveaways.

But who is the hired hand? And why would those slackers be allowed to watch the sheep if they are going to abandon the flock at the first sign of trouble? As temporary workers, it seems they're not really committed to the work and are watching sheep solely for the money. In today's world, there are pastors, broadcasters, authors, and musicians who may falsely present themselves as good shepherds. Their voice may even fool entire flocks. To protect yourself, seek and pray for discernment. Avoid such charlatans because they care nothing for the sheep.

GOING DEEPER:

Before leaving this passage, let's see if we can get a better handle on this promise that we *"may have life, and have it to the full."* That certainly could be a reference to the future glory in heaven promised to all believers. But the verse seems to present a hint of immediacy that implies we can find joy and rejoice in a life of meaning and significance here on this side of the threshold to eternity.

It comes down to knowing *who* you are and knowing *whose* you are. If you have turned from the destructive ways of the devil and received the gift of grace secured by Jesus on the cross, you will surely experience that abundant life promised in John 10:10. Your surrendered heart will be filled with gladness. *"Take delight in the* LORD, *and he will give you the desires of your heart"* (Psalm 37:4).

You know that Satan is the master deceiver. In your life, you have likely already seen and deflected many of his lies and scams. Still, you must stay alert because a hired hand may be your weak spot. Beware of those who say they know Christ but have no intention of protecting you from Satan. They may even be working to lure you away from God's love and plan for your life!

32

For I am not ashamed of the gospel, because it is the power of God that brings salvation to everyone who believes: first to the Jew, then to the Gentile.

—Romans 1:16

"For I am not ashamed of the gospel" is how Paul introduces himself via letter to the Christians in Rome. You may wonder why he felt the need to say he was *"not ashamed."* He certainly could have stated his commitment as a positive, such as, "I affirm the gospel" or "I proudly proclaim the good news of Christ."

This letter was written to lay the groundwork for Paul's upcoming trip to Rome. He knew there were factions in the city eager to disparage the name of Jesus as well as new believers who weren't yet confident in expressing their faith. Paul needed to emphasize the importance of dispelling any hesitancy, timidity, or shame when it came to proclaiming the gospel.

In addition, Paul was aware that the Jews saw Jesus as an obstacle, and the gentiles were disdainful of most religious practices. In 1 Corinthians 1:23, Paul explains, *"We preach Christ crucified: a stumbling block to Jews and foolishness to Gentiles."*

Specifically, the book of Romans is Paul's 16-chapter statement of faith, written to give a sample of what he would be preaching when he arrived in Rome: God is the sole source of life-changing salvation power. No action is required. Grace is a free gift available to everyone who believes.

Romans 1:16 is frequently memorized, and rightfully so. But typically the passage committed to memory stops before the end of the sentence: *"For I am not ashamed of the gospel, because it is the power of God that brings salvation to everyone who believes."* Did you ever wonder about the significance of the final words of the verse: *"first to the Jew, then to the Gentile"?*

Why did Paul determine that the Jews should take priority over the gentiles when it came to hearing the gospel? Probably because they knew the context!

The Jews had been waiting for the Messiah since God's promise to Abraham more than two thousand years earlier. Paul's ambition was to open the eyes of the Jewish people to the fact that Jesus was the conquering king promised in scores of prophesies in the Old Testament. Paul knew any Jew who received Christ would be a well-equipped and effective spokesman for the gospel. Focusing their initial outreach on the Jews was simply good strategy.

After Paul makes clear his stance on God's power found in the gospel, he communicates another revelation in the next verse:

For in the gospel the righteousness of God is revealed—a righteousness that is by faith from first to last, just as it is written: "The righteous will live by faith."
—Romans 1:17

In the Old Testament, God's chosen people saw activity as the way to get right with God, including burnt offerings and annually shedding the blood of livestock. But the ultimate sacrifice made by Jesus Himself on the cross eliminated the need for such activities once and for all. Hebrews 10:4 confirms this new covenant: *"It is impossible for the blood of bulls and goats to take away sins."*

Thanks to the events on Calvary, becoming righteous—being in a right relationship with God—is possible by faith alone. From "first to last," from beginning to end.

GOING DEEPER:

The passage ends with this curious restatement of a verse originally written in Habakkuk 2:4: *"The righteous person will live by his faithfulness."*

Feel free to ponder long and hard on what it means to live by faith. The approach may be different for every believer, but one strategy might be to pursue a constant awareness of your grace-filled, justified condition. You have been saved! As a result, you have the ability to lift in prayer a sincere and straightforward request. *God, Your grace has given me new life through Your Son. It was a free gift, and I accept it wholeheartedly. Please make clear how I can bring You glory, and give me strength and courage to give my best gift of my new life back to You.*

> **We mustn't think of our faith as hard work. Because if it's a task, as humans on occasion we will fail. And then what? Instead, ascribe your sincere but imperfect faith tightly to God's faithfulness. As Charles Spurgeon said, "What a mercy it is that it is not your hold of Christ that saves you, but His hold of you!"[2]**

---

2. C. H. Spurgeon, "A Sermon (No. 7–8) Delivered on Sabbath Morning, February 11, 1855, by the Rev. C. H. Spurgeon at Exeter Hall, Strand.," The Blue Letter Bible, https://www.blueletterbible.org/Comm/spurgeon_charles/sermons/0007.cfm.

33

> *"For I know the plans I have for you,"*
> *declares the LORD, "plans to prosper you and not to harm*
> *you, plans to give you hope and a future."*
> —Jeremiah 29:11

The book of Jeremiah is overflowing with accusations and warnings to the people of Judah. They were continually breaking God's covenant and worshipping false gods, leading Jeremiah to write, *"Your wickedness will punish you; your backsliding will rebuke you"* (Jeremiah 2:19).

In the chapters that follow, using history, poetry, biography, and records of his sermons, Jeremiah initially expresses hope and urges the people to turn back to God. He's not surprised, though, when he finds himself reluctantly prophesying the destruction of Jerusalem. When that prophecy comes to pass, the people of Judah begin their 70 years of captivity in Babylon under King Nebuchadnezzar.

In chapter 29, Jeremiah includes a letter to the exiled nation containing instructions to continue on with their lives with activities such as building homes and having children, and even praying for the pagan Babylonian nation that has enslaved them. While 70 years is a long time, Jeremiah assures Judah that they will one day return to their ancestral home.

The often-quoted verse Jeremiah 29:11 was part of that letter. Even today, the assurance found in that verse inspires and comforts many believers. The promise of a return to prosperity and a hope-filled existence includes specific instructions found in the next verse:

Then you will call on me and come and pray to me, and I will listen to you. You will seek me and find me when you seek me with all your heart.
—Jeremiah 29:12–13

Anyone quoting Jeremiah 29:11 and looking forward to God's prosperous plan should be urged to keep reading because it turns out there are some follow-up assignments worth doing. The next two verses (v. 12–13) include short, basic words that aren't hard to understand: Call. Come. Pray. Seek. Find. With all our heart.

What's more, those simple concepts must be important as they are repeated over and over throughout Scripture, especially for those enduring a bit of adversity. *"Call on me in the day of trouble"* (Psalm 50:15). *"Come to me, all you who are weary"* (Matthew 11:28). *"Is anyone among you in trouble? Let them pray"* (James 5:13). *"Seek and you will find"* (Matthew 7:7).

The destruction of Jerusalem and burning of the temple was a landmark event in Jewish history, a long reminder that disobedience to God leads to destruction. But sin would not have the final word. It never does.

GOING DEEPER:

The entirety of chapters 30 and 31 of Jeremiah reveals how the promise of a *"hope and future"* would unfold through the restoration of Israel. The current generation would endure seven decades of exile, finally regaining their freedom and returning to Jerusalem only after Cyrus conquered Babylon. But after another half century or so, Jeremiah prophesizes an even greater restoration that is coming: true freedom emerging in the dawn of a new covenant.

"This is the covenant I will make with the people of Israel after that time," declares the Lord. *"I will put my law in their minds and write it on their hearts. I will be their God, and they will be my people. No longer will they teach their neighbor, or say to one another, 'Know the* Lord,' *because they will all know me, from the least of them to the greatest," declares the* Lord. *"For I will forgive their wickedness and will remember their sins no more."* (Jeremiah 31:33–34)

That new covenant, of course, would come with the birth of Jesus and the reality of God walking among us as a man. Jeremiah foresaw that God's laws would no longer be an oppressive list of rules written on stone tablets and passed from neighbor to neighbor and generation to generation. Instead, the Holy Spirit would place in our hearts a desire to know God, to love Him, and to follow His will for our lives.

Then, as promised in Psalm 103:11–12, *"For as high as the heavens are above the earth, so great is his love for those who fear him; as far as the east is from the west, so far has he removed our transgressions from us."* In the same way, God will remember our sins no more.

> **Even when you find yourself in exile, feeling hopeless and unworthy of love, know that God's love and forgiveness is the core of the new covenant. He has written this promise on our heart. Keep pursuing God with small steps and small words—Call. Come. Pray. Seek. Find—and you'll discover He has been preparing your hope and future the whole time.**

34

This, then, is how you should pray…
—Matthew 6:9

The first few words of Matthew 6:9 may sound familiar, but unlike many of the verses in this book, they are probably not a biblical quote you've spoken often or have on a refrigerator magnet or inspirational wall plaque. But you may be surprised to hear this is one of the clearest instructions given by Jesus.

These words are a center point of the Sermon on the Mount. In Matthew 6:5–8, Jesus has just presented His foundational strategies for how to pray. (1) Do not stand on the street corner, hoping people notice how awesome you are. (2) Your most focused and effective prayer is going to be done in secret behind closed doors. (3) Don't jabber and spew shallow, insincere words. (4) God already knows your deepest needs.

After those instructions, Jesus Himself delivers a model prayer. Matthew 6:9 begins, *"This, then, is how you should pray."* You surely know the rest of the verse and beyond:

Our Father in heaven, hallowed be your name.
—Matthew 6:9

Commonly referred to as "The Lord's Prayer," Matthew 6:9–13 covers everything you need to consider when praying to God. Your pastor could probably spend a month of sermons exploring the meaning of each phrase, but let's see what we can glean in just a page or so.

Our Father in heaven. The Creator of the universe wants a relationship with each of us. He's real, and He's living in a place of eternal glory. He sent Jesus. He sent the Holy Spirit. But God the Father, while omnipresent, hears your prayers in heaven.

Hallowed be Your name. Even God's name is set apart—holy. Just the mention of His name unleashes unstoppable power.

Your kingdom come, Your will be done. These are bold statements: God reigns. God's will triumphs. But they are also prayer requests. We are asking God to send His Son back for His triumphant return—soon. At the same time, we are surrendering our will for His. He knows what's best for us anyway.

On earth as it is in heaven. Heaven and earth are two different and distinct places, but God is in control of both. Humans can't even begin to understand how the world and universe we physically inhabit work. There's no way we can grasp the awesomeness of heaven.

Give us today our daily bread. This seems pretty straightforward, except we're not just asking for bread, and it's not just once a day. God supplies all our needs, from oxygen to sunlight to the way our brain turns squiggly lines printed on the pages of this book into ideas on how to read a favorite verse of Scripture in context. God's ongoing provision is His gift to us, which we can never repay.

Forgive us our debts, as we also have forgiven our debtors. This could be considered the launching point of the gospel. We must acknowledge our brokenness and ask for God's forgiveness before the blood of Christ can wash away our sins. Once we understand the critical nature and power of forgiveness, then we will also follow God's example. But our job is much easier than His: all we have to do is forgive those who have wronged us, one person at a time. We can't begin to compare that to God's promise to forgive all the sins of all the people throughout history who believe and trust in Him.

And lead us not into temptation, but deliver us from the evil one. To be clear, God would never lead us into temptation, but He did give us free will, which means He *allows* us to be tempted. We need to ask Him to save us from ourselves. The request to deliver us from evil pinpoints the urgency. Satan is real, and we can't face him alone.

For Yours is the kingdom and the power and the glory forever. While this isn't included in every Bible version, we often finish the prayer with this phrase, which makes its intent come full circle. He's our Father in heaven, and His glory will last forever. He is the Alpha and the Omega.

Amen. Amen.

GOING DEEPER:

If you grew up in a home that rattled off the Lord's Prayer quickly and by rote, try slowing it down. Even though you likely have the entire prayer memorized, word for word, there's value in considering every word and phrase, every image and invocation.

Authentic prayer should be sincere and originate from the heart. With that goal, some believers suggest—or even insist—memorized prayer is ineffective. Since it's possible to say the words without thinking about them, some might even say any rote prayer is offensive to God.

That conclusion might be a bit of an overstatement. It's true that we don't want to be *"babbling like pagans"* (Matthew 6:7). But Jesus did say, *"This, then, is how you should pray."* That leads me to conclude the words that follow should be considered the perfect model of a perfect prayer for any believer.

Jesus presented the Sermon on the Mount early in His ministry on a hillside along the Sea of Galilee. (See Matthew 5:1–7:29.) Large crowds had begun to follow Him and were amazed at His teaching and His "healing every disease and sickness among the people" (Matthew 4:23). Later, perhaps with only the disciples as an audience, He delivers what might be called a "shorter version" of the Lord's Prayer. Skeptics might point to that version (Luke 11:2–4) as a contradiction in Jesus's instructions on prayer. Instead, you might consider those two renditions to be a reminder that exact words are not nearly as important as our persistence in prayer and God's faithfulness.

35

Am I my brother's keeper?
—Genesis 4:9

The story of Cain and Abel is actually not primarily one of sibling rivalry. It's a story about free will and how God is completely aware of every circumstance, sees our heart, and knows the future, but He still allows each of us to choose our own destiny.

As the story goes, Cain tills the soil and presents fruits of his labor as an offering to God, but they are rejected. Cain becomes angry. What makes it even more irritating for Cain is that God readily accepts a gift from his little brother, Abel. Genesis doesn't say specifically why Cain's gift wasn't worthy. But we get a hint when we read that Abel's gift was *"fat portions from some of the firstborn of his flock"* (Genesis 4:4). Maybe Cain skimped, selfishly saving the best fruit for himself. Maybe he was testing God to see what he could get away with. Maybe Adam never taught his oldest son the importance of sacrificial giving.

Whatever the case, God speaks directly to Cain, *"Why are you angry? Why is your face downcast? If you do what is right, will you not be accepted? But if you do not do what is right, sin is crouching at your door; it desires to have you, but you must rule over it"* (Genesis 4:6–7).

How did Cain respond to this straight talk from God? He got even angrier. That happens sometimes when a person is caught red-handed. In essence God was saying, "Do what is right. Or else." God added a warning about the dangerous and ever-present power of sin. He was telling Cain that he still had the capacity to squelch his anger and flee temptation.

At that point, Cain could have backed down and chosen a fresh start. Instead he rejects God's instruction, lures his little brother out to a field, commits the first murder, and finds himself in another confrontation with the Almighty. "*Where is your brother Abel?*" God asks (v. 9). Cain's reply—versions of which are still spoken today whenever someone fails to take responsibility for their actions—is "*Am I my brother's keeper?*"

In the moment, God doesn't directly answer the question, but He does assess guilt and immediately begins to lay out His righteous judgment in the next verse:

The Lord said, "What have you done? Listen! Your brother's blood cries out to me from the ground."
—Genesis 4:10

Pronounced guilty, Cain can't say he wasn't warned. Neither can we. Most of us will never have a direct conversation with the Creator of the universe like Cain did, but we do have mentors, pastors, church families, small groups, friends and family, the power of prayer, and the leading of the Holy Spirit to help us use our own free will to make choices that honor God and give Him glory.

We have the story of Cain and Abel—and the entire Old and New Testament—to serve as guidance and a warning. Does Cain's punishment for the choices he made seem overly severe? The next two verses pick up where Genesis 4:10 leaves off:

Now you are under a curse and driven from the ground, which opened its mouth to receive your brother's blood from your hand. When you work the ground, it will no longer yield its crops for you. You will be a restless wanderer on the earth.

(Genesis 4:11–12)

To many, that punishment may seem like "something out of the Old Testament that really doesn't apply today." Unfortunately, deciding this no longer applies is just wishful thinking. The same punishment is still on the books. As a matter of fact, anyone who doesn't accept God's free gift of grace is under a curse, their work will not yield the success they seek, and their time on earth will be purposeless and devoid like a restless wanderer.

GOING DEEPER:

Cain's decision probably shouldn't be blamed on Adam and Eve, especially since God Himself had given Cain clear instructions. Parents of adult children need to be reminded that they are not directly responsible for any problematic decisions made by their grown kids. On the other hand, the disobedience of the first couple did escort sin into the world. Just a chapter earlier, Eve succumbed to the temptations of the serpent, Adam ate of the forbidden fruit, and both were banished from Eden forever. If we don't learn from our mistakes, we are doomed to repeat them.

Despite all these curses being delivered in the opening pages of the Bible, it's important to remember that God's love never ends. He is always waiting and willing to forgive. Still, He also cannot allow sin to go unpunished, and sin often has natural repercussions that last longer than we realize.

The LORD is slow to anger, abounding in love and forgiving sin and rebellion. Yet he does not leave the guilty unpunished; he punishes the children for the sin of the parents to the third and fourth generation.   (Numbers 14:18)

Free will is a gift. Like all gifts, we have the choice to use it for good or evil. We have the choice to create a future of blessings or curses for ourselves and those we love.

Twice, Cain had the chance to do the right thing, but didn't. His first negative choice—trying to pass off a few second-rate vegetables as an offering—was a minor infraction. God called him on it and warned that even greater sin was creeping closer and ready to pounce. Cain's next sin was murder, confirming that the choices we make can be a slippery slope. One sin leads to another. But one good deed also leads to another. The choice is ours.

36

Submit to one another out of reverence for Christ.

—Ephesians 5:21

The apostle Paul wrote these words to the church at Ephesus and to all followers of Christ in the first century and today. He challenges every believer to have the heart of a servant and put the needs of others first. It's a brilliant strategy for a healthy church. Submitting to one another creates a sense of give-and-take, a kind of reciprocity, that encourages each of us to look out for those in our circle and make sure everyone in the body is taken care of.

It's not a coincidence that the following passage transitions immediately to God's plan for marriage because strong families are the building blocks of a healthy church, community, city, and world. "Mutual submission" is a direct assignment spelled out here for all believers, but it's especially valuable within families. Some pastors may balk at the term, but it's a pretty accurate paraphrase of how the Bible describes a successful marriage. (See verses 22–33.)

So that we cover all three elements of a family—wives, husbands, children—we're going to look at not one, but several verses that follow. One of the most controversial statements both in and out of the church in recent years is the next verse:

Wives, submit yourselves to your own husbands
as you do to the Lord.
—Ephesians 5:22

If you're a wife reading this devotional, please don't slam this book shut and toss it in the dust bin. I assure you, any radical feminist who insists this verse is intolerable hasn't really considered the entirety of what it says. If you're hesitant to buy into the concept of this verse, simply ask yourself, *Why do I trust and submit to the Lord?* The answer is, because He loves you and cares deeply about your well-being.

Well, that's the same reason you can trust and submit to your husband. As best as is humanly possible, your husband loves you and cares deeply about your well-being. If that's not the case, then that's another story. But if the man you married is devoted to you, it makes perfect sense to encourage him to lead.

With that mindset, read Ephesians 5:22 again, and it might not seem so oppressive. It may even feel empowering to realize that both God and your beloved spouse are looking out for your very best.

Men, in the same way, you also need to earnestly read your own assignment that comes a few verses later.

Husbands, love your wives, just as Christ loved the church
and gave himself up for her.
—Ephesians 5:25

Husbands, did you hear your marching orders? Your wife needs you to take a leadership role, but you need to lead with love, specifically sacrificial love. Just as Christ gave His life for us, you need to willingly give your life for your bride. What does that mean? It might be something dramatic like holding back an army of marauding ninjas or fighting off a bloodthirsty porcupine. But more likely, it will be something not quite as exciting, yet much more important—that is, loving your wife sacrificially, putting her well-being before your own when it comes to your time, energy, resources, creativity, and even your will. It entails loving her as much as Jesus loves His followers.

By the way, gentlemen, if you intentionally and openly love your wife in this manner, it will be much easier for her to obey Ephesians 5:22.

This all works because men and women have different needs. Men need to lead, protect, and provide. Women need to feel valued and cherished. This brings us to the younger generation in the family. The idea of submitting to one another is also demonstrated when parents relinquish their will to meet the deepest needs of their children. As it turns out, children need...instruction! You can read it for yourself by skimming down a few more verses:

Children, obey your parents in the Lord, for this is right.
—Ephesians 6:1

Personally, I like the fact that the word "*obey*" is saved for the kids. In Ephesus and in your hometown, it's still okay for parents to expect obedience from the next generation.

GOING DEEPER:

While this book is not a marriage manual, the Bible does have much to say about romance, respect, fidelity, and love. For the record, there is no place in the Bible where it specifically tells women to "obey your husbands." "Love, honor, and obey" were once part of the wedding vows, but you won't hear "obey" at many contemporary ceremonies.

Further controversial passages on the topic of marriage and romantic love worth exploring would be 1 Peters 3:7, 1 Corinthians 11:3, Hebrews 13:4, and just about all of Song of Solomon. It is important to explore the intent of these verses instead of getting hung up on the vocabulary, like "submit."

Ephesians 5:21–6:3 is all good news for families. If you're a husband, please don't loudly grunt Ephesians 5:22 or use the words "submit" or "submission" to demand your own selfish motives. It should be undeniably evident that the idea of wives submitting to their husbands does not give any man permission to impose verbal or physical abuse.

38

He said to them, "The Scriptures declare,
'My Temple will be called a house of prayer for all nations,'
but you have turned it into a den of thieves."
—Mark 11:17 NLT

If you get over-the-top angry once in a while, then you are probably a big fan of Mark 11:15–19 and all the other Gospel references depicting Jesus getting loud, overturning tables, and even wielding a whip against the money changers in the temple.

When you stomp around, get loud, put your fist through walls, and fire off rage-filled tweets and posts, you don't feel guilty at all. After all, you're just doing what Jesus did. I understand the point you're making, but let's see if your position stands up to further scrutiny.

First, you have to admit that you don't have the authority of Jesus, the Son of God. He was defending *"my Temple."* He also had a sinless character, allowing Him to point out the sins of others aggressively without a hint of hypocrisy.

Second, Jesus had established Himself as the Prince of Peace. His primary recommendation when confronted with evil is to "turn the other cheek." (See Matthew 5:39.) In the Sermon on the Mount, He praised the merciful, the meek, and the peacemakers. The rage Jesus exhibited clearing the temple was profound and potent because it was not His typical behavior. Can you say that?

Third, Jesus knew what the response would be from the Pharisees. It's right there in the next verse.

When the leading priests and teachers of religious law heard what Jesus had done, they began planning how to kill him. But they were afraid of him because the people were so amazed at his teaching.
—Mark 11:18 NLT

When Jesus was born, His destiny to sacrifice Himself on the cross for our sins was already written. (Actually, it had been established before the beginning of time.) But in the eyes of the world, Jesus clearing the temple was when the *"teachers of religious law… began planning how to kill him."*

Jesus's rage in the temple launched the events that would save humankind. That's pretty important stuff. Now compare that with what happens when you rage. Does it change history? Does it even manage to change anyone's opinion? Or does it make you look foolish on Facebook? Does it embarrass your spouse or your kids? Before raging, we would do well to consider what the outcome of our rage might be.

Let's say you are justifiably angry about an issue that breaks God's heart, something horrific like abortion, human trafficking, slavery, or pedophilia. If there's a legitimate chance your action will make a difference, then get loud. Sometimes that's the only way to make your voice heard. But also consider there may be other options. Perhaps an option with less volume, but more impact. Write a letter. Write a check. Run for office. Volunteer. Pray. Go on a short-term mission project. Invite an adversary for coffee. Lead a small group. Teach Sunday school. Go to law school.

Tuck your kids in at night. Love your spouse. Adopt. Volunteer for foster care. Or here's an idea: formulate commonsense and biblical arguments and be prepared to deliver them with poise and respect.

Another effective strategy that could be employed more frequently by people who call themselves Christians is to live a life so exemplary and honorable that nonbelievers seek your advice.

No matter what, be very sure about your motivations and the ramifications of your actions before you storm into a building and start overturning tables. Consider the mandate of 2 Timothy 2:15: *"Do your best to present yourself to God as one approved, a worker who does not need to be ashamed and who correctly handles the word of truth."* In other words, don't be a Christian who brings shame to the body of Christ. Know the truth and handle it correctly.

GOING DEEPER:

The Bible also says, *"In your anger do not sin"* (Ephesians 4:26). That's an excellent warning. But it also confirms there is a kind of anger that is not sinful, perhaps even a force for good.

How can we make sure we limit our anger to the righteous kind? We need to take our own human limitations out of the equation. This requires us to focus not on our own issues, but instead to ask, "What makes God angry?" In James 1:19–20, we read, *"Take note of this: Everyone should be quick to listen, slow to speak and slow to become angry, because human anger does not produce the righteousnessthat God desires."*

Mark 11:18 ends with, "But they were afraid of him because the people were so amazed at his teaching" (NLT).
Notice, Mark is emphasizing that Jesus's words, not His miracles, amazed the people. This may be a little surprising, but it's good news to us mere mortals. We may not have Jesus's instant access to miracles, but we can use the same tools He used to bring wonder. Don't you think carefully chosen words have a better chance of being amazing when spoken with love, not yelled in anger?

38

For all have sinned and fall short of the glory of God.
—Romans 3:23

I confess, studying more about this verse and the next verse surprised me. (Together, they also confirm that the idea behind this book is valid.)

I'm not sure about you, but Romans 3:23 is etched into my brain. I wouldn't call it a favorite verse. After all, who wants to think about billions of people over the course of history—including you and me—sinning innumerable times during their lives and falling short of God's standards?

However, it is a short and memorable verse with a message critical for every person on the planet to understand. And it's ubiquitous. Any curriculum teaching the basics of the gospel must cover this concept and likely uses this verse from Romans. Millions of grade-school children have been taught Romans 3:23 in Awana, Kids4Truth, Royal Rangers, Christian Service Brigade, and dozens of other Bible-based curricula, and they are almost always encouraged to memorize those 11 words.

It's as foundational as John 3:16, *"For God so loved the world that he gave his one and only Son, that whoever believes in him shall not perish but have eternal life."*

It's as theologically essential as Romans 6:23, *"For the wages of sin is death, but the gift of God is eternal life in Christ Jesus our Lord."*

It's as historically accurate as 1 Corinthians 15:4, "*That he was buried, that he was raised on the third day according to the Scriptures.*"

These verses—and a handful more—can be recited word for word by many of the readers of this book. At least, that's what my publisher tells me.

Personally, Romans 3:23 is often top of mind. In a relatively casual conversation, when I'm trying to make a point about the broken state of our culture today, I may interject a paraphrased version of that perceptive verse simply to explain why we should not be surprised that the world is so messed up.

For example, if the topic turns to popular movies, I might say something like, "It's getting harder and harder to find a well-made film that doesn't have some creepy agenda or foul language. But what should we expect? Making movies is a business, and they're just trying sell tickets. Hey, all have sinned and fall short of the glory of God. There aren't a lot of Christians in Hollywood, and we shouldn't expect folks who don't know Jesus to act like they do."

If you follow my logic, you'll see I'm not attempting to evangelize. I'm just applying logic to explain why people commit immoral acts. We're all sinners, and sinners sin. After making a statement like that, the conversation either ends quickly or gets real interesting.

That being said, here's the reason for my surprise about Romans 3:23–24. In a way, there's nothing remarkable about these verses. If I came across those two verses during some routine Bible reading, I would have breezed by them. Their meaning is clear and is covered elsewhere in Scripture. I would definitely not have had a reason to look up Romans 3:23 in any study Bible or Bible app. Its meaning was never a mystery.

Also, until writing this book, I just took it for granted that it was embedded in the middle of a longer passage on sin, the dangers of sin, and the penalty for sin.

Instead, I was treated to a one-two punch of sin and mercy. The clarity and universality of Romans 3:23 is equaled in the next verse:

And all are justified freely by his grace through the redemption that came by Christ Jesus.
—Romans 3:24

All sin. All fall short. All are justified. All are freely redeemed by grace.

I hope it hits you the same way it hit me. For believers, it's not new information. Perhaps hundreds of passages say the same thing. But I so appreciate how the universal dilemma of verse 23 finds an immediate solution in verse 24.

GOING DEEPER:

Going deeper would lead us to a long conversation about justification, propitiation, redemption, sanctification, and glorification. Frankly, after basking in the simplicity of Romans 3:23–24, that would just make my head hurt. But if you're up for that kind of study, the remainder of the book of Romans covers all those big words. Have your Bible dictionary and favorite commentary handy.

Romans 3:23–24 parallels the old joke formula that begins, "A doctor walks in and tells the patient, 'I've got good news and bad news...'" While I hope you acknowledge the bad news that there is sin in your life, I also hope you have heard and accepted the gospel, the good news of Jesus Christ. Based on the passages found in this chapter alone, you have all the information you need.

39

The LORD will fight for you; you need only to be still.
—Exodus 14:14

Normally, we can be confident quoting Moses. One of the great heroes of the faith, his impressive credentials include receiving the Ten Commandments, leading the Israelites through the desert for four decades, and writing the first five books of the Bible. But this quote—specifically the second half of Exodus 14:14—may include instructions that are flat out wrong.

Extensive research resulted in exactly zero Bible scholars endorsing this theory, so I may be the one who is dead wrong. In any case, please indulge me as we invest a few paragraphs to explore this idea.

First, let's recall the dramatic and familiar scenario. After witnessing (and instigating) ten devastating plagues, Moses leads two million Israelites out of Egypt. Even though they are being led by pillars of clouds and fire, they still find themselves wandering in confusion. As Pharoah's army descends, they are blocked by the Red Sea. Predictably—and perhaps understandably—they howl to Moses.

> *What have you done to us by bringing us out of Egypt? Didn't we say to you in Egypt, "Leave us alone; let us serve the Egyptians"? It would have been better for us to serve the Egyptians than to die in the desert!* (Exodus 14:11–12)

Moses responds with an admonition to not be afraid, to stand firm, and to expect God to deliver them from the advancing Egyptian army. Then he delivers the often-quoted promise, "*The* LORD *will fight for you; you need only to be still.*"

In general terms, the two declarations in this verse are true. Yes, the Lord will fight for His people. Yes, sometimes we need to be still in order to hear the voice of God. But here's the often-over-looked point. In this particular case, God immediately contradicts Moses in the next verse:

Then the LORD *said to Moses, "Why are you crying out to me? Tell the Israelites to move on. Raise your staff and stretch out your hand over the sea to divide the water so that the Israelites can go through the sea on dry ground."*
—Exodus 14:15–16

As I read it, God is saying to Moses and the Israelites, "Quit your whining and get moving," which is the *opposite* of being still. Then God gives Moses specific instructions on how He will gain glory through the parting of the sea and describes the aftermath of what happens to Pharaoh's horses, chariots, and horsemen.

It's a good thing God overruled Moses. If the Israelites had followed Moses's instructions to be still, they would soon have been slaughtered at the water's edge, and all of human history would have been sidetracked.

Exodus does go on to explain how the angel of God moves the pillar of cloud between the Egyptian army and the cowering Israelites, protecting them for the night. At the same time, Moses actively follows God's instructions, stretches out his hand, and the Red Sea parts, allowing all two million escaping slaves to go "*through the sea on dry ground*" (Exodus 14:22).

As morning nears, the now confused Egyptian army follows the fleeing Israelites but soon realizes the Lord is, indeed, fighting against them. Before they can retreat, Moses again stretches out his hand, the water flows back, and *"not one of them survived"* (Exodus 14:28).

We think of Moses as a veteran leader with great experience and wisdom. But the parting of the Red Sea occurred fairly early in his career as a leader. He had been in communication with God at the burning bush and had told Pharaoh, "Let my people go." But it was in the crucible of escaping Egypt and being corrected by God (on several occasions) that he learned to trust God and became the leader we recognize today.

GOING DEEPER:

The longer and more keenly you study the Bible, two things that seem contradictory happen. First, you realize the Bible comes with inconsistencies, unexplained controversies, theological debates, gaps in time, and assertions that just don't seem logical. Second, you trust it more.

Consider the story in this chapter as an example: As recorded in Exodus 14:14, Moses may have been giving the Israelites instructions that God had to overrule: "Be still. Do nothing. Let God work His miracle." Or Moses could have been saying, "Be still for just one moment and God will give us marching orders that you can trust, but you won't believe." Either way works.

Enemies will attack. Whether God wants us to be still or take immediate action, we need to remember the first part of Exodus 14:14. God's weapons and battle plans are endless. He may vanquish our foes right before our eyes or sustain us in secret. He may protect us with a preemptive strike before Satan's attack even takes place. Or God may allow us to suffer for a season and rescue us in the nick of time. Be confident that Moses had that part right: "The Lord will fight for you."

40

This is my command: Love each other.
—John 15:17

Perusing the Bible, we come across all kinds of apparent promises regarding the power of love. Most of them seem to be self-serving, but in a good way. Others are about evangelism and encouraging others. *"Love each other"* is a short command, but it contains a bunch of benefits.

Love makes Christianity attractive. John 13:35 reveals, *"By this everyone will know that you are my disciples, if you love one another."* Christians who demonstrate love, kindness, and compassion will always be more effective in their outreach than those with some clever and cagey strategy for evangelism.

Love covers sins. First Peter 4:8 tells us, *"Above all, love each other deeply, because love covers over a multitude of sins."* Such a promise prompts follow-up questions: Does love prevent future sins or does it make up for sins of the past? Or possibly both? In any case, loving others makes us more aware of our own shortcomings as well as the needs of others, all of which causes us to sin less often and less severely.

Love squelches fear. First John 4:18 says, *"There is no fear in love. But perfect love drives out fear, because fear has to do with punishment. The one who fears is not made perfect in love."* When we accept God's love and allow it to overflow in our lives, there is no room for fear. We can be confident because Jesus took our punishment on the cross.

Love prevents isolation. Ecclesiastes 4:9–10 reminds us that *"Two are better than one, because they have a good return for their labor: If either of them falls down, one can help the other up."* Throughout history, authentic followers of Christ have been the first to follow the example of the Good Samaritan.

Love proves your salvation. First John 4:20 says, *"Whoever claims to love God yet hates a brother or sister is a liar. For whoever does not love their brother and sister, whom they have seen, cannot love God, whom they have not seen."* Hate has no place here.

Love is our response to Calvary. Romans 13:8 explains, *"Let no debt remain outstanding, except the continuing debt to love one another, for whoever loves others has fulfilled the law."* Of course, we can never compare the value of our love to the supernatural love of God and the sacrifice of His Son. But we need to keep trying to follow His example in our actions.

Being loved by God confirms that your citizenship is in heaven. The world is going to do the opposite of love. When you feel disturbed or dragged down by the ways of the world, take comfort in Jesus's words in the next verses:

If the world hates you, keep in mind that it hated me first.
If you belonged to the world, it would love you as its own.
As it is, you do not belong to the world, but I have chosen you
out of the world. That is why the world hates you.
—John 15:18–19

There's a giant leap between John 15:17 and the next two verses. Initially, Jesus is endorsing human love. The command in that verse confirms that Jesus is able and willing to supply every believer with the capacity to love, one person at a time.

Then in John 15:18–19, Jesus acknowledges the world's ability and propensity to hate, specifically directing that hatred toward Christians. He treats it as a fact. "The world" described here that hates Jesus and you does not include every member of the human race, although it can feel that way. It's only those who don't know grace.

The hatred advanced by the world makes it all the more imperative that believers understand and participate in the rewarding and life-giving act of giving and receiving love.

GOING DEEPER:

If the half-dozen reasons to be loving listed above leave you unmotivated, perhaps you need some benefits that are a bit more self-serving. First Peter recommends you have unity of mind, love tenderly, display empathy, turn the other cheek, and be a blessing for purely selfish reasons.

> *Finally, all of you, be like-minded, be sympathetic, love one another, be compassionate and humble. Do not repay evil with evil or insult with insult. On the contrary, repay evil with blessing, because to this you were called so that you may inherit a blessing.* (1 Peter 3:8–9)

It may feel a lot more satisfying to repay evil with evil, but revenge is not ours to give. We should leave that to God. He's got more experience and also has that lake of fire waiting for evildoers. As for us, if we go against our first instinct and respond to evil with love, there's a very good chance we may obtain a blessing!

Loving others should not be difficult. It should not be something that strains against our will. Our love for others should come naturally out of our relationship with Christ and

the indwelling of the Holy Spirit. If you dare, you might even do some serious self-evaluation in the spirit of 1 John 14:20 (referenced above) to discern your capacity to love and test to see whether or not you are truly saved.

41

I have hidden your word in my heart that
I might not sin against you.
—Psalm 119:11

Psalm 119 falls close to the middle of the Bible. With 176 verses, it's the longest chapter in the Bible. Psalm 119 is actually an acrostic poem divided into 22 stanzas, with each stanza beginning with a letter of the Hebrew alphabet.

While many of the psalms feel like an emotional crying out to God in worship, praise, celebration, despair, gratitude, and repentance, Psalm 119 adds an overarching instructional tone. Almost every verse mentions the Bible itself, using synonyms like "law," "word," "precepts," "decrees," "statutes," "commands," "truth," and "promises."

Psalm 119:11 is one of the most memorized verses in all of Scripture. That's a bit ironic (or meta) because, of course, the verse is asserting that the writer has memorized Scripture.

The process of hiding God's Word in your heart is a worthy pursuit. Specifically, it could mean choosing a passage and committing it to memory word by word and verse by verse. Or it could mean choosing a passage, reading it, meditating on it, considering the context, and applying the precepts to your life.

In either case, once you claim a portion of God's Word as your own, you'll discover that it has the power to remind and warn you about sin and temptation lurking around the next corner. Equally as valuable, God's Word reminds you of the benefits of obedience. Once you see the big picture of how God can work in your life, you are more likely to stay close, pursue His will, and avoid even the appearance of sin.

The second acrostic stanza in Psalm 119 begins with a question: *"How can a young person say on the path of purity?"* (v. 9). After this question, the author launches into a handy list of recommendations for proactive ways to put God's Word to good use, including hiding it in your heart (v. 11). Don't miss additional strategies found in the surrounding verses:

How can a young person stay on the path of purity?
By living according to your word. I seek you with all my
heart; do not let me stray from your commands. I have
hidden your word in my heart that I might not sin against
you. Praise be to you, LORD; teach me your decrees. With
my lips I recount all the laws that come from your mouth.
I rejoice in following your statutes as one rejoices in great
riches. I meditate on your precepts and consider your ways.
I delight in your decrees; I will not neglect your word.
—Psalm 119:9–16

Before unpacking all the answers to the question posed in Psalm 119:9, let's consider the validity of the question itself: *"How can a young person stay on the path of purity?"* A few follow-up questions will bring clarity.

+ Is purity a worthy goal?

+ Is purity a one-time decision or a path that needs to be followed every day?

+ What happens when an individual wanders from that path?

+ Does this journey really pertain only to young people?

All are excellent questions, but not particularly difficult to answer. Once we define purity as being free from sin, we realize that it's not so much a destination as an ongoing process. We can seek righteousness. We can flee immorality. But in the end, our human weakness requires us to rely constantly on God for grace and forgiveness. We cannot stand against impurity on our own. Which brings us back to the question posed in Psalm 119:9: *"How can a young person stay on the path of purity?"*

One answer is well-established: memorize Scripture, hide God's Word in your heart. But there's more. Psalm 119:9–16 clearly provides us with a list of choice active verbs: Live. Seek. Do not stray. Hide. Praise. Be taught. Recount. Rejoice. Meditate. Consider. Delight. Do not neglect.

In other words, memorizing Scripture is just one of many ways to interact with Scripture. Apply all of these activities and God's Word will not only impact your life, but the lives of everyone you meet.

GOING DEEPER:

Psalm 119 is a love story to the Bible. Spend an hour with all 22 of the stanzas or paragraphs and you'll discover some new insights and warnings such as: *"It was good for me to be afflicted so that I might learn your decrees"* (Psalm 119:71) and *"The wicked have set a snare for me, but I have not strayed from your precepts"* (Psalm 119:110).

You'll also find some favorite and familiar verses. *"How sweet are your words to my taste, sweeter than honey to my mouth!"* (Psalm 119:103) and *"Your word is a lamp for my feet, a light on my path"* (Psalm 119:105).

Memorizing verses of the Bible may seem unnecessary in today's world. After all, you may have a dozen Bibles in your home, and Bible apps are a click away on your smartphone. But the value is not simply being able to access a verse or quote it verbatim. It lies in having the truth of Scripture penetrate your heart and soul.

In cultures where Christians are persecuted for their faith, stories abound of those in prison meditating on passages they had previously memorized and even sharing them with fellow prisoners. Their cherished Bibles had been confiscated and destroyed, but their testimonies reveal their very survival was only possible because they found courage and strength in God's Word, which they had hidden in their hearts.

42

Give me neither poverty nor riches,
but give me only my daily bread.
—Proverbs 30:8

There's only one prayer in the entire book of Proverbs, and it was written by a prophet most Christians have never paid much attention to named Agur.

As you know, most of the book of Proverbs was written by Solomon or perhaps his minions. The last chapter in Proverbs was written by King Lemuel and contains that sometimes controversial description of the "wife of noble character."

Proverbs 30 was written by an amusing and peculiar fellow about whom we know very little. He introduces himself as a weary, ignorant brute. His writing style delivers a hint of satire, sounding almost like a standup comedian who specializes in observational humor. The chapter includes five quirky lists in which Agur ponders things like how eagles fly, snakes slither, and lizards scamper through palaces. Agur reveals his true nature as a prophet when he mentions that God will have a Son, a revelation that is rare in the Hebrew Bible.

The gist of Agur's prayer is that our sweet spot lies somewhere between poverty and riches. That's where we find our daily bread, and *only* our daily bread—no more or less than we need.

I so appreciate this verse. As soon as I first became aware of it, Proverbs 30:8 became one of my favorites.

Beyond his humility and comedic sensibility, I also appreciate Agur's self-awareness. He knows that materialism is his weakness. After his clear prayer for *"neither poverty nor riches,"* he explains the reason behind his prayer in the next verse:

Otherwise, I may have too much and disown you and say,
"Who is the LORD?" Or I may become poor and steal, and
so dishonor the name of my God.

—Proverbs 30:9

Agur knows that if he has too much, his ego will take over and he will take all the credit for his success. He also knows that if he has too little, he will turn to thievery, which would reflect negatively on his role as a prophet.

Agur is endorsing moderation, which is not on anyone's checklist, especially in the 21st century. We live in an age of extremes. Bigger is better—more house. More car. More closet space. More shelves for more trophies. More activities so you can complain about being "so busy."

On the flipside is another extreme. There is another part of the subculture choosing to live as minimalists, cutting up credit cards and clearing out clutter. They eschew the latest gadgets. Their entire wardrobe fits in one knapsack or cardboard box. They're considering moving into one of those micro apartments or tiny homes.

Proverbs 30:8–9 offers a better option: seek balance. This concept can be applied to many of life's pursuits. Let's give Agur credit because he is conscious of where he might veer off course. His attitude regarding "stuff" is his stumbling block. This leads to a question for all of us. What endeavors or desires have you bouncing off the guardrails of life?

Besides materialism and cash flow, your stumbling block might be related to work, exercise, food, hobbies, lawn care, shoes, or any number of obsessions keeping you from finding your sweet spot.

Next time you find yourself living in the extremes, consider turning to Proverbs 30:8–9 and praying the only prayer in all of Proverbs, the prayer of Agur.

GOING DEEPER:

Often in Scripture, the term "bread" refers to daily provision. Written in the time of Solomon's reign as the third king of Israel, Agur's request for daily bread would have reminded any of his peers of the daily manna God had provided to their ancestors as they wandered the desert for 40 years. As described in Exodus, manna appeared once a day, provided by God in just the right amount at just the right time. If the Israelites gathered more manna than they needed, it would spoil. Isn't that true of so many things today?

As 21st-century readers, we recognize the phrase "give us this day our daily bread" from the Lord's Prayer, delivered almost a thousand years later by Jesus in His Sermon on the Mount. The words are comfortable, and we nod our heads. *Yes, Lord, please meet our daily needs.* The thing is, that's not what Agur prayed. He added the word *only*. "*Give me only my daily bread.*"

In God's sweet spot, the pressure is off. You can be sure it's all going to work out. You can move forward to explore life, secure in your relationship with the Creator of the universe. When you find yourself panicking over worldly successes or failures, it's reassuring to know God loves you no matter what. This is true when you're on a winning streak or when you're hurting. When you're seeking His face or turning away. Whether your cup is empty or overflowing. The fact that God loves you just as you are is the truest thing about you.[3]

---

3. Adapted in part from *The Prayer of Agur* (pp. 36–45, 75–76), ©2020 by Jay Payleitner, Multnomah, a division of Penguin Random House LLC.

43

No one can serve two masters. Either you will hate the one and love the other, or you will be devoted to the one and despise the other. You cannot serve both God and money.
—Matthew 6:24

The Bible has around 500 verses concerning faith and approximately 500 on the topic of prayer. But it contains more than 2,300 on money and possessions! Here are just a few:

For the love of money is a root of all kinds of evil. Some people, eager for money, have wandered from the faith and pierced themselves with many griefs. (1 Timothy 6:10)

For where your treasure is, there your heart will be also. (Luke 12:34)

Whoever loves money never has money enough; whoever loves wealth is never satisfied with their income. (Ecclesiastes 5:10)

We can certainly make the case that money itself is morally neutral. It's not evil. It's not virtuous. It's merely a resource, a tool that can be used for good or evil, and that's our choice. Still, so often money is tied to human emotions, including greed, anxiety, appreciation, envy, relief, surprise, fear, and worry.

That could be why—right after the Bible clearly states that the pursuit of possessions will distract you from pursuing God—the topic of worry comes up in the next verse:

Therefore I tell you, do not worry about your life, what you will eat or drink; or about your body, what you will wear. Is not life more than food, and the body more than clothes?
—Matthew 6:25

The familiar verses that follow confirm that God takes care of the birds of the air and the lilies of the field, which should prove that He is going to care for our needs. This rich passage (no pun intended) continues with the reminder, *"Can any one of you by worrying add a single hour to your life?"* (Matthew 6:27).

Admittedly, this entire idea of being unconcerned regarding our well-being here on earth is difficult and even a little confusing for hardworking and productive breadwinners in today's world. Worry seems to come with the assignment of caring for our family and others. We have mortgages to pay and mouths to feed. We want to put a few bucks in the basket on Sunday mornings and maybe take an occasional vacation and retire someday. All that takes cash. Plus, the Bible does encourage hard work: *"Those who work their land will have abundant food, but those who chase fantasies have no sense"* (Proverbs 12:11).

Maybe that's the point. Chasing superfluous stuff and agonizing about some kind of fantasy future is what nonbelievers do. The takeaway might be that a worry-free life comes from putting first thing first. Matthew 6:33 says, *"Seek first his kingdom and his righteousness, and all these things will be given to you as well."*

GOING DEEPER:

Perhaps the way to think of money is this: It's important and valuable, but financial wellbeing is a gift. Every nickel is a resource we've been given to be used wisely. It's also different for every person. Money comes and goes. Logic tells us we can sharpen and increase our brainpower, muscles, creativity, ability to communicate, appreciation for art and music, construction skills, common sense, and many other abilities and talents. In the same way, we should be working to strengthen and increase our effectiveness with the money we do have. But worry is almost always counterproductive.

Finally, let's acknowledge a few thoughts this chapter may have inspired: *If God is going to take care of our every need, why should we plan for the future? Or save? Or even work? Also, why should we give to those who are less fortunate? Won't God take care of them?*

While you mull over your own answer to those questions, consider these healthy approaches to our work and finances:

Meeting our needs is a promise from God, so we should ask ourselves how He has gifted each of us to meet our own needs, thereby fulfilling God's promise.

Our work helps align our perspective with God's. As we are made in His image, within our human limitations, we should dare to create and be as productive as He is.

By working diligently six days, we honor and better enjoy the gift of the Sabbath.

When it comes to the needs of others, we are often the tools God uses to make a difference.

Our priority as Christians is to listen for God's call and be ready to serve, which requires us to stay healthy and have the resources to respond.

I leave you with this warning: it's been said that money, tithing, and financial insecurity have caused more believers to stumble than any other issue.

Money can accomplish a lot, but there is a list of things that are more important than money and aren't for sale at any price. Open your Bible to the Fruit of the Spirit (see Galatians 5:22–23) and you'll immediately see that you cannot place a dollar value on love, joy, peace, patience, kindness, goodness, faithfulness, gentleness, or self-control.

44

All the believers were united in heart and mind.
And they felt that what they owned was not their own,
so they shared everything they had.... There were no needy
people among them, because those who owned land or
houses would sell them and bring the money to the apostles
to give to those in need.
—Acts 4:32, 34–35 NLT

It's inspiring to read about the first days of the Christian church. Those early believers were all of one mind and one heart. They shared everything. Miracles abounded.

The second chapter of Acts describes a compelling and magnetic environment. The emotionally charged day of Pentecost brought violent winds and tongues of fire that rested on the disciples. Peter, who had exhibited some wishy-washy tendencies in the Gospels, somehow spoke boldly, *"urging all his listeners, 'Save yourselves from this crooked generation!' Those who believed what Peter said were baptized and added to the church that day—about 3,000 in all"* (Acts 2:40–41 NLT).

There's a utopian feel about what's going on. It's pretty easy to endorse the feeling that *"what they owned was not their own"* (Acts 4:32 NLT). But a clarification is needed. There was, in fact, ownership of property; plus, the sacrificial sharing we see is not mandatory, but voluntary. Peter, John, and the rest of the leadership team did not put the squeeze on landowners. This was not some kind of forced socialism.

At the time, the idea of specific spiritual gifts being given to each individual at the moment they received Christ was being realized and revealed for the first time. Later, Paul would assemble a series of lists to define them. (See 1 Corinthians 12:4–11, 1 Corinthians 12:28, and Romans 12:6–8.) One of those spiritual gifts was generosity, and an individual with this gift would demonstrate not only how to be generous, but also the benefits to all involved. His story begins in the next verse.

> *For instance, there was Joseph, the one the apostles nicknamed Barnabas (which means "Son of Encouragement"). He was from the tribe of Levi and came from the island of Cyprus. He sold a field he owned and brought the money to the apostles.*
> —Acts 4:36–37 NLT

This passage shows we need to give Barnabas credit for leading the way as a model of generosity. Giving land was not a requirement of belonging to this movement in and around Jerusalem. Nor was giving everything you had. But Barnabas, mindful of those in need, sold off one of his properties and trusted the apostles to distribute those funds to those other followers of Christ in need. This would be just the first example of how he would be an encourager, thereby earning his nickname.

GOING DEEPER:

Barnabas is a recurring hero in the book of Acts. You could even say he was a key catalyst for much of the New Testament.

After his shining example of generosity, Barnabas shows up again when the recently converted Saul tries to join forces with the disciples. Not surprisingly, the believers wanted nothing to do with Saul, who had gained a reputation as a frenzied persecutor of Christians.

When [Saul] came to Jerusalem, he tried to join the disciples, but they were all afraid of him, not believing that he really was a disciple. But Barnabas took him and brought him to the apostles. He told them how Saul on his journey had seen the Lord and that the Lord had spoken to him, and how in Damascus he had preached fearlessly in the name of Jesus. So Saul stayed with them and moved about freely in Jerusalem, speaking boldly in the name of the Lord. (Acts 9:26–28)

Without Barnabas's advocacy, "Saul" might never have become "Paul." The apostles may never have trusted their former enemy without Barnabas's encouraging words.

Later still, in Acts 11:22–30, Saul and Barnabas teamed up for an entire year in Antioch. At that growing church, gentiles were becoming believers and, unlike Jews, who knew the history and teaching of past generations, these gentiles were mostly biblically illiterate. The two missionaries saw the need to stay on as patient teachers and encouragers. Of note, the first time disciples were called "Christians" was at Antioch.

Another time Barnabas's encouragement gave a boost to the growth and expansion of the new church was when he gave John Mark a much-needed second chance. The young missionary had unexpectedly gone AWOL on an earlier trip with Paul. (See Acts 13:13.) Preparing for a later journey, Barnabas made the case for John Mark's involvement, but Paul disagreed. The two long-time missionary partners parted company and subsequently two teams were formed: Barnabas sailed to Cyprus while Paul headed through Syria and Cilicia. In God's design, perhaps twice as much ground was covered and twice as much outreach accomplished.

The initial passage above makes the case for unity and integrity and meeting the needs of fellow believers around you. But the bigger picture points to the story of Barnabas in which we gain a new appreciation for spiritual gifts, generosity, advocacy for those who need your endorsement, keeping your eyes open for the needs of others, and giving second chances, as well as how God can work even through a disagreement of long-time friends.

45

For to me, to live is Christ and to die is gain.
—Philippians 1:21

In just a few words, Paul confirms what could be the two most compelling realities of the Christian life. First, living out the gospel should be a joy-filled existence. Second, we need not fear death because heaven awaits.

In addition, within that loaded statement lies a question: Which is preferable? Living on earth with a purpose or the unimaginable joy of being face to face with Christ in the next life? It's a win-win. Both actually are rewarding choices. But the answer, of course, is option two. Heaven is way better! *"To die is gain"*!

But hold on. As a servant leader and someone who has realized the satisfaction of putting others first, maybe it's better—for now—to remain in this life and complete the work of recruiting more disciples.

Attempting to draw an earthly analogy, here's one way to look at it. Let's say you have a dozen longtime friends—high school teammates, college classmates, the old street gang, or some other pals from the past. You have been recruited to track them down for an all-expense-paid reunion at a fabulous resort. If you don't have any phone numbers or emails, you could go all by yourself and have a nice relaxing time. But what if you contacted four of them? That could be a fun trip, right? Or should you hold off and see if you can round up the entire crew?

That question hints at the dilemma Paul is facing. He knows his mission: to round up as many friends (and strangers) as possible. He also knows his joy would be increased. The more the merrier, right? So whatever it takes to bring more people to paradise is worth the effort, even if it means delaying the trip.

He presents this choice as a struggle in the next verse:

If I am to go on living in the body, this will mean fruitful labor for me. Yet what shall I choose? I do not know!
—Philippians 1:22

Actually, I don't think he is struggling. In the next few verses, Paul restates his quandary, but quickly reveals that he has already made up his mind.

I am torn between the two: I desire to depart and be with Christ, which is better by far; but it is more necessary for you that I remain in the body. Convinced of this, I know that I will remain, and I will continue with all of you for your progress and joy in the faith, so that through my being with you again your boasting in Christ Jesus will abound on account of me.
(Philippians 1:23–26)

The church at Philippi had been a joy to work with ever since being founded during Paul's second missionary journey. Paul writes the entire letter to thank them for their love and partnership and to confirm that God will continue to work in them and through them.

You have to wonder what choice Paul would have made if the Philippian church had been less about joy and more about rules, rivalry, selfish ambition, or gaining notoriety. Maybe he would have prayed, "Lord, my work here is done. Take me home."

Instead, he gladly told the joy-motivated church on the Aegean Sea (in what is now northern Greece) that he is going to stick around and keep boasting in Jesus. There's a lot of joy in this uplifting letter, which, by the way, was written from a jail cell.

GOING DEEPER:

Hang around a variety of churches long enough or kick around Christian-themed websites, and you'll hear someone quote Philippians 1:21–22 and suggest that Paul was contemplating taking his own life. It's almost as if Paul's words are being equated with Hamlet's infamous question from act 3, scene 1 of Shakespeare's play bearing the character's name: "To be, or not to be: that is the question." The Bard may have had Philippians 1:21 in mind when he wrote the play. But in any case, the hypothesis that Paul was suicidal doesn't hold water.

Paul didn't have a death wish; he had a life wish! He wanted to squeeze every drop out of his life. As stated above, he answered his own question almost immediately. More likely, it was a question he put out there for the Philippian church to mull over. This letter of encouragement and the question he proposed was his way of confirming that he did not fear death, and neither should they. At the same time, he needed to confirm loud and clear that doing God's work here on earth is an even more urgent priority.

This passage in Philippians is also Paul's way of saying, "If you're not ready to die, you're not ready to live."

One other motivation for Paul's question was his precarious legal situation. At the time he sent this letter, we don't know whether any judge in Rome had sentenced him to a short or long sentence or even death. The meaning of life vs. death was top of mind for Paul, and he had time to ponder the implications. Isn't it inspiring that he saw God's love and perfect plan in both options?

46

When I consider your heavens, the work of your fingers,
the moon and the stars, which you have set in place,
what is mankind that you are mindful of them,
human beings that you care for them?
—Psalm 8:3–4

The imagery and lyrical quality of these verses draws you in. You can imagine God sweeping His hand across the vast darkness to establish the galaxies. That singular action—which actually occurred at the dawn of history—is the very definition of "awesome." Then, we are blown away and completely humbled by the idea that the Creator who has that kind of power cares for us. Compared to Him, we are nothing. It seems impossible that He loves and treasures each and every person who ever lived. But that's how He works.

That's a healthy perspective. In case you didn't catch all that, allow me to paraphrase Psalm 8:3–4: "There is a God. And you're not Him."

This seems self-explanatory. Unfortunately, there are quite a few folks who have an inflated sense of their worth. Even people who call themselves Christians sometimes have an aggrandized view of themselves. They look in the mirror and see a sterling citizen quite worthy of being God's favorite.

People with that kind of spiritual pride need to commit (or recommit) to having the heart of a servant. Obeying God is part of the obedience, responsibility, and reverence required of all believers. In Luke 17:10, Jesus puts that expectation into words: *"So you also, when you have done everything you were told to do, should say, 'We are unworthy servants; we have only done our duty.'"*

The Bible doesn't say that any Pharisees were within earshot when Jesus was teaching this lesson to the disciples. But that's exactly the kind of reminder that would have spoken to their high-and-mighty nature. Compared to everything Jesus did for the human race, we are assuredly unworthy.

While Psalm 8:3–4 needs to be read and memorized by those suffering from spiritual pride, those who are thinking too poorly of themselves really need to embrace the next two verses:

You have made them a little lower than the angels and
crowned them with glory and honor.
You made them rulers over the works of your hands;
you put everything under their feet.
—Psalm 8:5–6

Did you hear that? If you're trudging through life discouraged or embittered, believing you have no purpose and no value, think again. God has crowned you with glory and given you dominion over the world. Every place you walk is in your charge.

The opposite of spiritual pride is thinking you're unworthy of God's love. In many ways, such thinking is equally damaging and dangerous. If you don't think God can use you, you'll never reach your potential in Christ.

Getting specific, you have more to offer than you can imagine. You hold the power to love, give, weep, smile, heal, encourage, instruct, comfort, and so much more. Your most important job is to identify your gifts and discern how, where, and when they should be used.

As a born-again believer, you have been given much. I hope you realize that. At the same time, don't think too highly of yourself or assume that you deserve the gifts you have received because of your own efforts. Remember, God's angels still outrank you.

GOING DEEPER:

Knowing your place in the universe is critical to your ability to bear fruit. You're not God. You're not an angel. You're not an animal. You're not dust. As a matter of fact, your worth can be found in Jesus. He traded His life for yours on the cross. Martin Luther called this "the great exchange," whereby our sin is taken on by Jesus and the earned righteousness of Jesus is credited to all who call upon the name of the Lord.

Humbly accepting that gift and knowing your identity in Christ is really an easy choice.

> **If you want to think big thoughts and pursue big dreams, go outside on a clear night and ponder the stars. In Genesis 15, it worked for Abraham, who famously received the promise that his descendants would number as the stars. Looking up at God's handiwork, you'll feel small and vastly empowered at the same time. You may not literally hear God's voice, but then again, you might!**

47

So I say to you: Ask and it will be given to you; seek and you will find; knock and the door will be opened to you.
—Luke 11:9

Undoubtedly, you are familiar with some or all of Luke 11:9. Sometimes you hear it, say it, or see it one phrase at a time: *"Ask and it will be given to you," "Seek and you will find,"* or *"Knock and the door will be opened to you."*

One could make the argument that they all say the same thing. Repetition—especially words, phrases, ideas, and teachings repeated three times—is a common occurrence in the Bible. This is used sometimes for emphasis, sometimes for historical confirmation, and sometimes to help us consider a lesson from a different perspective.

In Revelation 4:8, the winged creatures drive home an important point about God's character when they repeat, *"Holy, holy, holy is the Lord God Almighty."* In Luke 15 we find successive parables of the lost sheep, lost coin, and lost son that pretty much all make the same point. The four Gospels repeat most of Jesus's teaching two, three, or four times. Even Luke 11:9 is echoed in Matthew 7:7.

But closer consideration of what it means to "ask," "seek," and "knock" will reveal that these are three different steps with three different results.

Before you can properly ask, you need to have a justifiable reason for asking. Are you hungry? Anxious? Broken? Are you in need of a little help as you work toward a worthy, well-thought-out goal? Asking is easy. Knowing why you are asking takes a bit more effort.

Seeking requires action. It's about keeping your eyes open as you pursue a worthy objective. It's about planning your search strategy and peeking around corners. However, it's still a solo activity.

Knocking is a bit more aggressive and gets a second party involved. The goal is for someone to hear that knock and respond.

Applying these three strategies to your prayer life, you can see that you can't just stop with your initial halfhearted attempts to get God's attention. He hears your request. He sees you seeking. He listens for your knock. Mostly, He appreciates your perseverance. By the time you get to step three, your persistence has confirmed your desires and has helped focus your own heart and mind on the part you need to play in receiving the answer to prayer. Plus, your resolve will help you to be aware of how and when God starts to respond on your behalf. Also, there's a chance that, through prayer, your will and desires may change. Mostly, though, the time it takes to ask, seek, and knock provides an opportunity to gain perspective and align your prayers with God's will.

How does this play out in real life? Luke 11:9 is actually the moral or takeaway from a parable told by Jesus about the value of perseverance. He tells the brief story in the preceding four verses:

> Then Jesus said to them, "Suppose you have a friend,
> and you go to him at midnight and say, 'Friend,
> lend me three loaves of bread; a friend of mine on a
> journey has come to me, and I have no food to offer him.'
> And suppose the one inside answers, 'Don't bother me.
> The door is already locked, and my children and I are in bed.
> I can't get up and give you anything.' I tell you, even though
> he will not get up and give you the bread because of
> friendship, yet because of your shameless audacity he will
> surely get up and give you as much as you need."
> —Luke 11:5–8

Jesus weaves a parable that makes the case for persistent prayer. Prayer with a purpose. Praying any time. Praying with expectations. Praying on behalf of someone else. And even, it seems, being a little obnoxious in your prayer. The unexpected permission to have *"shameless audacity"* is only possible because God knows your true motivations and loves you without condition.

This perseverance comes from counting on Him, which is a good thing. Just as God can handle when you are angry or filled with doubt, He can also put up with your chronic requests even when they sound like demands.

GOING DEEPER:

Keep reading in Luke chapter 11 and you will find the verse that compares God to earthly fathers.

> Which of you fathers, if your son asks for a fish, will give him a snake instead? Or if he asks for an egg, will give him a scorpion? If you then, though you are evil, know how to give good gifts to your children, how much more will your Father in

heaven give the Holy Spirit to those who ask him!

(Luke 11:11–13)

Taken in its entirety, Luke 11:5–13 reminds us that God is a loving provider who wants to hear from us and will provide exactly what we need. What will that be? It won't be snake or scorpion. But it also might not be exactly what you ask for. It could be something even better, it could be the removal of some thorn in the flesh, or it might be grace and strength sufficient to get through this season of life. In any case, keep asking, seeking, and knocking.

> **You can't read Luke 11:9 without thinking about a similar verse in Revelation 3:20: "Here I am! I stand at the door and knock. If anyone hears my voice and opens the door, I will come in and eat with that person, and they with me." But the verses are the exact opposite! In the Gospel, we are doing the knocking. In the last book of the Bible, Jesus is knocking. I recommend you keep that door to your heart unlocked and ajar. When He knocks—and He will—run and open it wide.**

48

Cast all your anxiety on him because he cares for you.
—1 Peter 5:7

What burden are you carrying? A temporary illness, an incurable disease, financial woes, a rocky marriage, fallout from a nasty divorce, a child with learning disabilities, teenagers making bad decisions, a job you hate, neighbors with barking dogs, a lack of friends, estranged family members, anger issues, abandonment, abuse, post-traumatic stress disorder, obsessive-compulsive disorder, feeling invisible, addiction, depression, confusion, tech anxiety, impossible deadlines, insomnia, chronic pain, acne, bullying, anorexia, bulimia, overcommitment, parental expectations, or any number of fears from agoraphobia to xenophobia.

The two-part verse 1 Peter 5:7 gives you a clear instruction and backs it up with the reason why that instruction works. First, hand over those fears and anxieties to God. Ask Him for relief. Second, trust Him. He loves you and cares for every part of your life.

The above list of woes is long and includes challenges that may be well served by human intervention. Solutions may include physicians applying God's gift of modern medicine, therapists trained in biblical counseling, career counselors, financial planners, coaches, or teachers. Authentic Christian friends, siblings, parents, pastors, coworkers, and others can come alongside you with words and physical comfort motivated by love without charging anything.

Cast your cares on God. Trust that He cares for you. But part of that process is looking for resources that He has already made available to you. You have to do your due diligence. We must also heed the warning in the next two verses:

Be alert and of sober mind. Your enemy the devil prowls around like a roaring lion looking for someone to devour. Resist him, standing firm in the faith, because you know that the family of believers throughout the world is undergoing the same kind of sufferings.
—1 Peter 5:8–9

Once again a passage of Scripture that seems like it is taking all the burden off your shoulders is followed by a passage saying you've still got a bit of work to do.

Hang tightly to 1 Peter 5:7, but approach your anxieties with open eyes and a clear mind. The specific burden that comes to mind when you read this verse is a weak spot and prime target for Satan's attack. Identifying it and giving it to our loving, caring God provides a much-needed layer of protection. In other words, by casting your cares on the Lord, you will have new capacity to do what it says in the next two verses—be alert, resist Satan, and stand firm in faith.

The rarely mentioned bonus of all this new empowerment may be the most rewarding revelation in this passage. You are not alone. God cares for you. But you have a "*family of believers throughout the world*" who are experiencing your same burden. I'm not sure why, but knowing that others are going through the same thing makes it a lot easier, doesn't it?

In summary, put God in charge of your greatest anxiety and expect some level of physical, emotional, and spiritual healing. God may send you to a resource available in this world He created to find your solution. No matter what, resist the temptation to give into any false doctrine, pity party, self-destruction, blame game, or denial that Satan might be offering. While you're at it, go head and specifically pray for a believer—a friend or stranger—going through a suffering similar to yours. There's a good chance they may be praying for you.

GOING DEEPER:

Even when a believer considers making an appointment with a pastor or professional Christian counselor, they would do well to double down on prayer and the application of biblical principles. *"Be alert and of sober mind."* You may never consider walking into a new-age storefront that sells healing crystals or promises a path to enlightened self-discovery, but you might very well be fooled by someone sent by Satan that looks safe and says all the right things.

An additional warning in Colossians 2:8–9 confirms that the world is constantly coaxing even the most devout believers away from the faith: *"See to it that no one takes you captive through hollow and deceptive philosophy, which depends on human tradition and the elemental spiritual forces of this world rather than on Christ."*

Be alert, sober minded, and prayerful, and stand firm so that you can resist Satan in all his forms.

Sometimes we can trace our heaviest burdens back to our own sin and foolish choices. This can lead us to believe that we deserve what's dragging us down. In our imperfect human condition, we do make mistakes that lead to suffering for ourselves and others. But God still cares about every part of our lives. He wants us to turn to Him.

49

So whether you eat or drink or whatever you do,
do it all for the glory of God.
—1 Corinthians 10:31

Giving God glory always feels good. If you've just had a well-deserved success, there's something deeply satisfying about thanking God for giving you the opportunity, gifts, and ambition to perform at a high level.

A full heart overflowing with joy and appreciation can be present whether you just were awarded a blue ribbon for your pickles at the county fair, landed a corner office at work, won an Oscar for your screenplay, or skated to earn an Olympic gold. For an authentic Christian, these accomplishments are especially satisfying. You had the vision and you put in the work, but you humbly dedicate your achievement to the One who made it possible. Nonbelievers never feel the privilege of giving glory to God.

But that's not what 1 Corinthians 10:31 is talking about. Paul was writing to the church at Corinth not about their great victories, but about how they should respond to the corruption and immorality of the society around them.

Earlier in the passage, Paul clarifies some confusion and addresses a conflict going on in the church regarding the new freedom found in receiving Christ. In 1 Corinthians 10:23–30, Paul explains the idea that some things might not be sinful, but they

The Next Verse 181

could cause others to stumble or doubt. For example, an action that seems harmless might upset brothers and sisters who still appreciate some of the old Jewish traditions.

One way to look at our responsibilities as a member of the body of Christ is to affirm the truth of John 8:36: *"If the Son sets you free, you will be free indeed."* But before we go wild and crazy with that news, we need to realize there are things equal to or more important than our freedom, things like love, the gospel, the welfare of others, and our own personal integrity.

That's the kind of thing Paul was talking about in the next two verses.

Do not cause anyone to stumble, whether Jews, Greeks or the church of God—even as I try to please everyone in every way. For I am not seeking my own good but the good of many, so that they may be saved.
—1 Corinthians 10:32–33

In his teaching on the wise use of our freedom as believers, Paul unravels any confusion regarding ancient rules on sacrificing to idols and how certain food and drinks can be sold and consumed. But mostly his point is one that has application for today. Your words and actions should give God glory and not cause someone to doubt their faith or put them in the path of possible sin.

One obvious example of creating a stumbling block is making liquor easily available to a struggling alcoholic. Another example would be giving children access to certain movies, books, and music. Disparaging other denominations or pastors might cause a seeker to doubt the entire Christian faith. Driving erratically with a Christian bumper sticker might not be a sin, but it doesn't help build the kingdom. If you choose to hold hands around the table and pray at a public restaurant, you should also make a point to leave a generous tip.

GOING DEEPER:

Earlier translations of 1 Corinthians 10:23 included the phrase, "Everything is permissible for me," and it's easy to see how that could be misconstrued or misused to justify forbidden activities. Here's a current popular—and more accurate—translation: "'I have the right to do anything,' you say—but not everything is beneficial. 'I have the right to do anything'—but not everything is constructive."

Beyond 1 Corinthians 10:23–33, there are other passages that contain warnings on causing another to stumble, including Romans 14:13 and 1 Corinthians 8:9–13. These are worthwhile reminders to Christians that the world is watching us. What nonbelievers see should make them want what we have. A quote attributed to William J. Toms says it well: "Be careful how you live. You may be the only Bible some person ever reads."

> **In a practical sense, the parallel is that just because something is lawful doesn't mean it's moral. As a matter of fact, Christians should rarely ask the question, "Is this lawful?" Instead, we should be asking, "Will this bring glory to God?" or "How will this impact my witness for Christ?"**

50

He fell to the ground and heard a voice say to him,
"Saul, Saul, why do you persecute me?"
—Acts 9:4

Saul chased down Christians like a bounty hunter, devoted to the task. He is first mentioned in the New Testament as a willing witness to the stoning of Stephen, the first Christian martyr.

It's not that Saul wasn't religious. Quite the opposite; he was a religious zealot. A well-trained and model Pharisee, he knew the Hebrew law and saw members of the Christian movement—who called themselves *The Way*—as a threat to Judaism. As far as he was concerned, this new cult worshipped a "mere" man as if he were God Himself! This was a provocation to everything Saul knew to be true.

Saul's persecution campaign had official paperwork giving him permission to target the synagogues in Damascus where he expected to identify members of The Way and take them as prisoners to Jerusalem. But God had other plans.

On the road to Damascus, a light from heaven flashed around Saul and he fell to the dirt, struck blind. Acts 9:4 documents the words heard by Saul and the men who were traveling with him: *"Saul, Saul, why do you persecute me?"*

Recognizing that this voice came from a deity of some kind, Saul responded in the next verse:

"Who are you, Lord?" Saul asked. "I am Jesus,
whom you are persecuting," he replied.
—Acts 9:5

The relatively short passage in Acts chapter 9 is the primary historical documentation of Saul's Damascus Road experience. Later in Acts, Saul—whose name would be changed to Paul—recounts additional details of the event.

As a prisoner accused of breaking Jewish law, Paul knew he had the legal right to speak, and he used his circumstances to gain an audience in Caesarea with the powerful King Herod Agrippa and various high-ranking officials. He chose to risk death by telling his story and making a clear presentation of the gospel.

In that powerful oratory recorded in Acts 26, Paul honors the history of the Jewish people, gives his personal history as a Pharisee and persecutor of Christians, describes his conversion experience in detail, and then relates how Jesus commissioned him as His messenger to the gentiles so they might turn from the power of Satan, move from darkness to light, and find forgiveness of sins.

The lessons from Paul's stunning conversion and courageous testimony are many:

- Making a U-turn in life is possible. God is still working miracles today. Don't give up on any of your loved ones—or yourself.

- Whatever you're passionate about, ask yourself, *How can God use that passion?* Paul was a religious zealot turned religious zealot!

- If God gives you an opportunity to tell your story—to any audience, large or small—be courageous in letting your faith shine through.

+ Finally, notice the question Saul asked after falling to the roadbed: *"Who are you, Lord?"* That's a question everyone needs to ask. Once you realize the truth, it changes everything.

GOING DEEPER:

Are you jealous of believers who talk about their "Damascus Road Experience"? I used to be. You see, I wasn't rescued from a life of obvious or outrageous depravity. I wasn't a bully, drunk, womanizer, addict, or thief. From early on, I was a pretty good churchgoing kid who in his mid-twenties finally realized his sinful condition and need of a Savior. My conversion story never made the evening news.

Pretty boring stuff, huh? Not to me it isn't! It turns out my mundane story is one that a lot of people need to hear because they can relate to it. On the outside, my life didn't change that much, but my motivations and view of the world were radically transformed, just like our friend, Paul.

That's the short version of my story. If you have a comparable conversion story, track me down at jaypayleitner.com and let me hear it.

> Why would the voice from heaven say, "I am Jesus, whom you are persecuting"? It was not Jesus, but people—members of The Way—who Paul was arresting and probably arranging to have killed. The answer is that Jesus sees believers as the body of Christ on earth. Even today, anyone who persecutes Christians is guilty of persecuting Jesus. This idea should drive us to be even more compassionate and proactive regarding martyrs and persecuted believers around the world.

51

*In My Father's house are many mansions; if it were not so, I
would have told you. I go to prepare a place for you.*
—John 14:2 NKJV

As the story goes, every Sunday morning a certain pastor looks out
at his flock with an excess of sanctimony and thinks, *These are the
only people going to heaven.* This pastor suffers from tunnel vision
and believes every other person in the world who calls themselves
a Christian is getting it wrong. As a matter of fact, the pastor's
unwarranted judgment, extrabiblical policies, and insignificant
doctrinal discrepancies have chased away his entire flock except
for the 47 brainwashed sheep left in the pews.

That's an extreme example, but it's not farfetched. There are
absolutely truths worth dying for. Philippians 1:27 challenges us
to *"stand firm in the one Spirit, striving together as one for the faith of
the gospel."*

It's even true that the path to heaven is the road less traveled.
Jesus describes the exactitude required to make the journey. *"Enter
through the narrow gate. For wide is the gate and broad is the road
that leads to destruction, and many enter through it. But small is the
gate and narrow the road that leads to life, and only a few find it"*
(Matthew 7:13–14).

Please don't miss this point. Although the gate is narrow, it's
not difficult to squeeze through. The gospel is not burdensome.

Matthew 7:14 is simply saying there's only one gate, which is, of course, Jesus Himself.

There are people who think only their church, only their denomination, or only those who check off precise boxes and jump through certain hoops can be heaven bound.

The World Christian Encyclopedia suggests that the "six major ecclesiastico-cultural mega-blocs" account for more than 33,000 denominations.[4] Having so many options may sound to some like heresy and apostasy are running rampant. But perhaps it's good news! It turns out many of those denominations are independent churches or smaller enclaves of churches set apart by geography or culture. If those groups are faithfully preaching the core truths of the faith, that means there are thousands of pastors and churches reaching their community with the gospel.

That's a lot of people. And that's why Jesus confirms in John 14:2 that He has and will prepare many mansions for those making that journey through the narrow gate.

While humans can get bogged down in the pros and cons of denominations and theological questions that have been debated for centuries, Jesus doesn't. The One who opens the door and prepares the mansions prefers to focus on individuals. I'm so glad for the next verse:

And if I go and prepare a place for you,
I will come again and receive you to Myself; that where I am,
there you may be also.
—John 14:3 NKJV

---

4. David B. Barrett, George T. Kurian, Todd M. Johnson, eds., *World Christian Encyclopedia, 2nd ed.*(Oxford, et al.: Oxford University Press, USA, 2001), http://www. philvaz.com/apologetics/a106.htm.

These promises delivered not long after the Last Supper tell us that Jesus Himself is not only preparing our place in heaven, but He is also going to personally escort each and every one of us. Wow. This passage also confirms Jesus's itinerary. As Bible readers today, we know His plans, but several of His disciples may be just beginning to understand that Jesus will be crossing into or out of heaven three times.

John 14:3 tell us Jesus will "*go*," "*come again*," and "*receive*" us back to be with Him for eternity. This includes His ascension (see Acts 1:9–11), then the triumphant return (see 1 Thessalonians 4:16), and finally Jesus ushering to heaven all Christians who remain (see 1 Thessalonians 4:17 and Matthew 24:29–31).

We don't know the timing of these last two events, and many of the details of the second coming are up for debate. No matter how it works out, we have the promise from Jesus Himself that where He is, we will be also.

GOING DEEPER:

John 14 is one of those chapters in the Bible jampacked with welcome promises for all believers. For additional context, the above verses are bookended by some additional life-giving and often-quoted verses.

In John 14:1, Jesus continues his teaching in the upper room after the last supper, "*Do not let your hearts be troubled. You believe in God; believe also in me.*"

As the conversation after the Last Supper continues, we come to another unforgettable question and answer mentioned back in chapter 10 of this book. John 14:5 features Thomas sincerely asking, "*Lord, we don't know where you are going, so how can we know the way?*"

The response is one of the most revealing passages in all of Scripture: *"Jesus answered, 'I am the way and the truth and the life. No one comes to the Father except through me'"* (John 14:6).

You may have noticed that our key verses for this chapter are from a different translation. Frankly, it's because I just have this desire to stay in a heavenly "mansion." Most of the other translations say, "In my Father's house are many rooms." A mansion is cooler than a room, right? Tell you what, if you promise not to get bogged down in miniscule denominational differences, I will try to be satisfied with a mere "room" in heaven.

52

What shall I return to the Lord for all his goodness to me?
—Psalm 116:12

Across the entirety of the book of Psalms you'll be inspired to praise God as Creator, express gratitude for His love and provision, ask forgiveness, bask in His glory, and turn to Him for care and comfort in your brokenness.

Read, study, memorize, pray, or sing Psalm 116 and you'll encounter all those emotions and realities. The opening lines feature familiar refrains found throughout the psalms referring to loving the Lord, hearing His voice, and calling out to Him. Two early verses get a bit graphic.

> *The cords of death entangled me, the anguish of the grave came over me; I was overcome by distress and sorrow. Then I called on the name of the Lord: "Lord, save me!"*
> (Psalm 116:3–4)

What happens when we call out, "Lord, save me!"? It turns out that's exactly what He is waiting to hear. God wants us to acknowledge our sinful condition and need for a Savior. He promises to come through for us: *"Everyone who calls on the name of the Lord will be saved"* (Romans 10:13).

That's a helpful promise to hang on to when entangled in cords of death or anguishing over the grave. When we are rescued, our natural inclination is gratitude, which generates a sincere desire to reciprocate. The question being asked in Psalm 116:12 is, "How should we respond?"

The psalmist acknowledges that he has been rescued by the goodness of God and attempts to find some way to give back to God. Then he answers his own question in the next verse:

I will lift up the cup of salvation and call
on the name of the Lord.
—Psalm 116:13

You have to believe the psalmist's sincere desire to somehow repay God for His goodness. But it may be impossible.

He asks a heartfelt question in verse 12, but his own answer in verse 13 seems almost hollow or superficial. All he offers is to lift up the cup of salvation and speak the name of the Lord. Those are nice thoughts, but the cup was a gift he apparently is re-gifting to the Giver. And calling on God is really just saying thank you again. Neither of those responses seem like much of a sacrifice.

On the other hand, maybe those two responses are exactly what God wants from us. He wants us to honor, cherish, and elevate the cup of salvation as the greatest gift in history. Think back to Jesus's prayer in the garden of Gethsemane. *"My Father, if it is possible, may this cup be taken from me. Yet not as I will, but as you will"* (Matthew 26:39). Although written centuries apart, Psalm 116 and Matthew 26 are referring to the same cup. Whether it's the Holy Grail of blood from the Last Supper or a metaphor for Christ's suffering and death, the cup has infinite value. Lifting it gives glory to God.

Calling on the name of the Lord does the same thing. It's a way to pray continually. It's a way to acknowledge we are His and share the good news with others.

You can't outgive God. He doesn't really need our help. He's delighted you dropped a half million dollars in the church offering basket last week, but He doesn't need your money. Psalm 50:10 reminds us that God owns the *"cattle on a thousand hills."*

GOING DEEPER:

There is nothing we can really give to the Lord for all His benefits to us. Our response can only be to receive what He gives us and then express our love, thanksgiving, and worship. Actually, the best way to make use of His gifts is probably to reinvest them in kingdom building.

Like the farmer who plants seeds, we should expect a harvest with any work we do pointing others to God. In 2 Corinthians, we read how God's provision allows us to reap a blessing of righteousness so that we can be generous, which results in even more gratitude to God.

> *Now he who supplies seed to the sower and bread for food will also supply and increase your store of seed and will enlarge the harvest of your righteousness. You will be enriched in every way so that you can be generous on every occasion, and through us your generosity will result in thanksgiving to God.*
> (2 Corinthians 9:10–11)

Whether it's seeds, money, service, love, your home, or any gift from God, you can show your gratitude by modeling authentic Christian faith as you lift up the cup of salvation and call on His name.

This area of theology can be tricky. Think of it this way: we are called to give to God not because it's what He needs, but because it's what we need. We need to hold loosely to anything in this world that we deem precious: our homes, family, careers, cars, money—any material things—are all temporary. The only things on earth today that will last for eternity are people and God's Word.

53

It is for your good that I am going away.
Unless I go away, the Advocate will not come to you;
but if I go, I will send him to you.
—John 16:7

At the Last Supper, Jesus patiently explains (or re-explains) many vital concepts of the Christian faith to His disciples, including the earth-changing events that would unfold over the following three days. Imagine the disciples' concern and puzzlement when Jesus reveals that He is going to the Father but will send *"the Advocate"* in His place. How could anyone possibly replace Jesus, their living, breathing, walking friend who taught and guided them with such clarity?

In John 16:7, Jesus calmed their fears and eased their grief by saying it is *"good that I am going away."* Then He goes on to explain how the Holy Spirit cannot make His appearance until after Jesus Himself departs.

As an aside—and perhaps sounding a little irreverent—that switcheroo always seemed to me a little like how Clark Kent had to leave before Superman arrived and vice versa. The analogy breaks down on many levels, including the fact that Jesus and the Holy Spirit have already been in the same place at the same time, most notably at Jesus's baptism (see Matthew 3:16).

The Holy Spirit goes by a variety of names across the Bible and differing translations, including Advocate, Counselor, Comforter, Paraclete, Spirit, Spirit of Truth, and others. The Spirit gives us access to the fruit of the Spirit as described in Galatians 5:22–23.

As Jesus explains to the disciples, the Holy Spirt will have a three-part mission that will bring clarity to all who are willing to listen. He begins to spell it out in the next verse:

When he comes, he will prove the world to be in the wrong about sin and righteousness and judgment.
—John 16:8

Of course, Jesus has already been speaking truth on the topics of sin, righteousness, and judgment. Along with His teachings, He's been putting His truth-filled words into action. Jesus paid the price for sin. He justified every believer with righteousness in the eyes of God. All along Jesus has been clear about the condemnation and judgment of Satan and those who reject the gospel.

As a man, Jesus had been modeling how to live. With His death, He completed His earthly mission, saying, *"It is finished,"* on the cross (John 19:30).

Then after His departure, as promised, the second chapter of Acts records the coming of the Holy Spirit at Pentecost, and Christians have been blessed by His supernatural guidance ever since. This new Advocate's purpose is to continue the work of the Messiah by equipping first the disciples and then all believers with the power to recognize right and wrong, convicting us when we fall short and empowering us to act boldly in the face of injustice or evil.

GOING DEEPER:

Every authentic Christian is guided every moment of every day by the indwelling of the Holy Spirit. Unfortunately, on too many occasions, most of us choose not to follow His counsel. What's more, if you find yourself unaware of any leading by the Spirit or discounting the negative impact of sin, you may want to assess your standing as a believer. Romans 8:14 counsels, *"For those who are led by the Spirit of God are the children of God."*

Believers can count on the Holy Spirit as an unending source of comfort, wisdom, intercession, and truth. All of these benefits should take away some of the sting that Jesus had to depart this world, at least for now.

One of the ways to know you are in tune with the Holy Spirit is to follow the fruit. On any given pathway in life, if you live by the Spirit, you already know that one way will lead to a dose of patience and peace, while the other leads to turmoil. Before you open your mouth, you already know that saying certain words will lead toward spite and regret, while others open the door to forgiveness and joy. If you're not sure how you're doing, ask your closest friends and family members. The ones who care about you will let you know how you're doing when it comes to love, gentleness, and self-control.

54

My grace is sufficient for you, for my power is made perfect in weakness.
—2 Corinthians 12:9

One of my Bibles is a red-letter edition, which means the words of Christ are printed in red. As I mentioned previously, I recommend everyone own a red-letter Bible because just skimming the words spoken by Jesus helps you realize that He is still speaking to us today.

As you can imagine, there's a lot of red in the Gospels, but not much in the rest of the New Testament. As a matter of fact, 2 Corinthians 12:9 has just a single sentence in red and that's the above 14 words.

Leading up to that passage in his second letter to the Corinthians, Paul challenges the members of the church (and us) to trust and depend on God. He acknowledges their trials, warns about false teachers, and even encourages generosity, *"For God loves a cheerful giver"* (2 Corinthians 9:7). Then, in a surprising turn, Paul begins to list examples of his own personal suffering, including prison terms, floggings, stoning, threats from bandits and his own countrymen, shipwrecks, hunger, sleeplessness, and more. (See 2 Corinthians 11:16–33.)

If you consider human nature, these defeats by a leading spokesperson for this growing faith movement could have been seen as a failure in the eyes of the world. Taken as such, those apparent setbacks could have led to a critical turning point for Corinth and other cities where the gospel was being preached. After all, no one wants to be associated with a loser. Even more disturbing, Paul caps off his list of hardships by disclosing his mysterious "thorn in the flesh" (2 Corinthians 12:7).

Paul's unidentified ailment has been a source of debate among pastors and scholars for centuries. Was it physical, spiritual, or emotional? A punishment or a gift? Since it's described as a *"messenger of Satan"* (v. 7), what was the message? Why did God allow it? Should Christians today expect some kind of "thorn in the flesh"?

Paul concludes that the unnamed ailment is a warning for him to stay humble in the wake of all the revelations he has been given. Still, he prays three times for the thorn to be removed and then documents Jesus's reply: *"My grace is sufficient for you, for my power is made perfect in weakness."*

Inspired by those words from Jesus, Paul doubles down on his boasting about the "thorn" and all his suffering, even revealing that he delights in his weakness—which brings us to this paradoxical statement found in the next verse:

For when I am weak, then I am strong.
—2 Corinthians 12:10

If you're following along, 2 Corinthians 12:9 is the words of Christ but verse 10 comes from Paul. With that one-two punch, it's reasonable to conclude there's no reason ever to whine, moan, or complain about your suffering. Both Paul and Jesus confirm that strength comes when you finally admit your best work cannot be achieved under your own power. That's especially true if your life is about pursuing Christ and advancing the gospel. Frankly, admitting your own shortcomings is the key to finding and getting the most mileage from the gifts you've been given.

Just to confirm, 2 Corinthians 12:10 is not referencing physical strength, although the idea of emotional and spiritual endurance is woven into this promise.

The essential takeaway here is the value of humility and applauding our dependence on God. He does bestow us with gifts and abilities—perhaps even giving us mad skills that make the world sit up and take notice. But if we start taking credit for our success, we will—sooner or later—be facing our own shipwreck or thorn in the flesh.

GOING DEEPER:

I think 2 Corinthians 12:10 is more than just about turning difficulties into victories. Scripture certainly corroborates the idea that God will turn your ashes into beauty, redeem lost years, and bring light to the darkness. But weakness is not something from which to be rescued. Weakness should be our goal. Weakness empties us so that we can be filled with God's power. It's central to the theme of redemption in the Bible: we cannot do anything with our own power.

While scholars have struggled with the idea, it may be that this passage confirms that even those events that are cheered by Satan can and will be used for good when God intervenes. That's how Christ claimed victory over torture and death on the cross. That's what enabled Joseph to speak so eloquently in the last chapter of Genesis when he reassures his brothers, *"You intended to harm me, but God intended it for good to accomplish what is now being done, the saving of many lives"* (Genesis 50:20).

That's why the words printed in red in 2 Corinthians pledge, "*Grace is sufficient.*" If you need a rallying cry for the day, try this: get weak for God!

Let's finish this chapter with a word game. Consider these oxymoronic statements and ask yourself if they are possibly true. Humility is what makes me awesome. Accepting my ignorance is what makes me wise. Asking for help is empowering. Being a servant makes me a leader. Finally, of course, "The last will be first, and the first will be last" (Matthew 20:16) and "Whoever wants to save their life will lose it, but whoever loses their life for me will find it" (Matthew 16:25).

55

*Now faith is confidence in what we hope for and assurance
about what we do not see.*
—Hebrews 11:1

Have you ever had someone say to you, "Well, you just have to have faith"? How did that sit with you?

The word itself is a little tricky to define and apply. *Faith* is most often recognized as a noun. Also, it doesn't necessarily have religious implications. For example, before climbing a ladder, you need to have faith it will support your weight. Confusion also comes because any system of religious beliefs can be called a "faith." Christianity, Buddhism, Gnosticism, and Rastafarianism are all faiths.

To a Christian, "faith" is pretty important. Ephesians 2:8 explains that it's a key link in the chain to salvation: *"For it is by grace you have been saved, through faith—and this is not from your-selves, it is the gift of God."*

Hebrews 11:1 is helpful as it closely links faith with confidence, hope, and assurance. That's true even if we can't clearly see or figure out every aspect of how faith works. What's more, there should be comfort and relief that we don't understand every motivation or capability regarding the Creator of the universe.

Applying the concept to real life, faith begins with having the knowledge of who Jesus is and what He accomplished through His death and resurrection. Then—secure in that knowledge—there needs to be an understanding of our own brokenness and a desire to be rescued from our sinful and imperfect condition. It's not something we can do on our own. Even our best efforts can't earn a passing grade. Finally, faith allows each of us, in a single moment, to make the choice to trust in what Jesus has done on our behalf.

We can make the case that faith is a tool used once in a single moment to gain salvation and all the accompanying benefits. But let's also recognize a second definition of faith as a resource we can develop and grow to help us better navigate life.

For real-life examples of how this works, we just need to consider the long list of historical biblical heroes of the faith introduced by the next verse:

This is what the ancients were commended for.
—Hebrews 11:2

After this set up, the remaining 38 verses of Hebrews chapter 11 deliver an impressive list of ancients who not only had faith but lived by faith. You're going to want to read the entire passage, and as you do, notice the words *"By faith"* are repeated more than a dozen times as they remind us of God's faithfulness to specific individuals whose names you recognize from the Old Testament.

By faith Abel brought God a better offering than Cain did.
(v. 4)

By faith Enoch was taken from this life, so that he did not experience death.
(v. 5)

By faith Noah, when warned about things not yet seen, in holy fear built an ark to save his family. (v. 7)

By faith Abraham, when called to go to a place he would later receive as his inheritance, obeyed and went. (v. 8)

The passage expands on life lessons from each of these men and continues with stories of the victories of Isaac, Jacob, Joseph, Moses, Rahab, and other prophets, martyrs, kings, and servant leaders all driven by faith.

Interestingly, the last two verses of the chapter serve as a reminder that even heroes may not enjoy the full fruits of their heroic deeds here on earth and, perhaps, an even more important victory comes as they pass the baton of faith to future generations.

These were all commended for their faith, yet none of them received what had been promised, since God had planned something better for us so that only together with us would they be made perfect. (Hebrews 11:39–40)

The Bible is filled with admonitions, instructions, and principles to live by. But after reading Hebrews 11, you have to admit that hearing how those truths can be lived out in the real lives of real people helps us realize that the principles are valid, not arbitrary. Faith makes sense. The Word works. The Bible is a road map for life.

GOING DEEPER:

Personally, I'm glad God exists beyond my puny human imagination. I can't see Him and that's okay. By faith, I believe there is a Creator God who loved me enough to save me from myself. That's why 2 Corinthians 5:7 makes perfect sense: *"For we live by faith, not by sight."*

But I am also glad that we have the role models in the pages of Scripture who have lived out their faith and led armies, built arks, passed through the Red Sea on dry land, hid spies, and more. What's more, if you look around, you'll see that role models still exist today. Maybe you're one yourself.

Faith is more than believing God exists. That's only step one. James 2:19 says it well: "You believe that there is one God. Good! Even the demons believe that— and shudder." The good news is that the power that makes demons shudder is on your side. Step two is trusting God with your life and surrendering it to Him. If you do this, your life will be given back to you with a bounty of freedom and purpose you can't imagine.

56

Draw near to God, and he will draw near to you.
—James 4:8 ESV

You have to love this soul-soothing, comforting thought. These words in James 4:8 tells us we can ease our way into God's presence, and while He is still out of our reach, He will close that gap with arms that are always open.

This idea is embodied in the parable of the prodigal son as he finally comes to his senses and shows up broken and feeling unworthy at the end of his father's driveway. Seeing his son, the father immediately runs to him! (See Luke 15:20.) In the same way, if we take a couple steps toward God, He will quickly approach us so we can reach Him.

How do we draw near to God? His omnipresence suggests He is already present wherever we are, so drawing near is not about narrowing some kind of physical distance. It could be about our attitude toward God. There are many reasons we might be keeping God at arm's length: fear, lack of trust, ignorance, a distorted image of who He is, past feelings of betrayal, or a desire for autonomy, among other unfortunate excuses. Maybe we aren't turning toward God because we don't know how.

If you've heard a few sermons or sat in a Sunday school class, you've already heard a few familiar strategies for getting closer to God: Pray. Read the Bible. Memorize Scripture. Find a good church. Join a small group.

That's all good stuff, of course. But let's list a few more strategies for getting closer to God you may not have considered or that you might apply with more intentionality.

Inhabit creation. *"The heavens declare the glory of God; the skies proclaim the work of his hands"* (Psalm 19:1). Sometimes just walking outside and witnessing His handiwork will take you lightyears closer to God.

Reflect on what He has done for you. *"Praise the Lord, my soul, and forget not all his benefits"* (Psalm 103:2). Instead of taking good things for granted or thinking we achieve anything on our own, let's give credit to God, which will in turn help us turn toward Him.

Love your enemies. *"Love your enemies and pray for those who persecute you, that you may be children of your Father in heaven"* (Matthew 5:44–45). You may not have realized it, but any hatred or aversion you have for others builds a wall between you and God.

Try music. *"Shout for joy to the Lord, all the earth, burst into jubilant song with music; make music to the Lord with the harp, with the harp and the sound of singing, with trumpets and the blast of the ram's horn—shout for joy before the Lord, the King"* (Psalm 98:4–6). Be part of a joyful chorus before the Lord. Play your favorite instrument. Sing old hymns or new praise songs. For many, that's where they meet God.

Pray alone. *"When you pray, go into your room, close the door and pray to your Father, who is unseen. Then your Father, who sees what is done in secret, will reward you"* (Matthew 6:6). Don't stop praying at the dinner table and saying bedtime prayers with the kids, but also find someplace you can pray in secret! The result will be a more intimate fellowship with God.

Get closer to Jesus. *"No one comes to the Father except through me"* (John 14:6). To get close to God, get to know His Son because Jesus is the way.

The above strategies for drawing near to God so that He draws near to you feel very doable and user friendly. But maybe you're ready for a little more difficult work as described in the next verse:

Cleanse your hands, you sinners, and purify your hearts, you double-minded. Be wretched and mourn and weep. Let your laughter be turned to mourning and your joy to gloom.

—James 4:8–9 ESV

Drawing near to God may require you to do what the prodigal son did and take a personal inventory of your heart, mind, and soul. *"Cleanse your hands"* and *"purify your hearts"* so that you are worthy of being in the presence of God. *"Mourn and weep"* that you have kept Him at a distance. The action steps laid out in James 4:8–9 will give you the courage to turn back to God and find your way home. Don't worry, nothing you uncover or confess will be a surprise to Him.

Turning again to the psalms, here's a prayer that will jumpstart your assignment: *"Search me, God, and know my heart; test me and know my anxious thoughts. See if there is any offensive way in me, and lead me in the way everlasting"* (Psalm 139:23–24).

GOING DEEPER:

Reading James 4:8–9, did you pause at the accusation that you might be double-minded? Are you being pulled two directions? Are you attempting to serve two masters? We know that doesn't work. Earlier in James is a wonderful passage for anyone who is holding back from trusting God because they lack wisdom, have doubts, or are "double-minded."

> *If any of you lacks wisdom, you should ask God, who gives generously to all without finding fault, and it will be given to you. But when you ask, you must believe and not doubt, because the one who doubts is like a wave of the sea, blown and tossed by the wind. That person should not expect to receive anything from the Lord. Such a person is double-minded and unstable in all they do.*   (James 1:5–8)

Why would we want our laughter to be turned to mourning or our joy to gloom? The answer is in James 4:10: "Humble yourselves before the Lord, and he will lift you up." When our head drops in humble recognition of how broken we are, God puts His hand under our chin, lifts our head, meets our eyes, wipes our tears, and tells us it's all going to be okay.

57

If God is for us, who can be against us?
—Romans 8:31

The word "if" is what your high school English teacher would call a conditional subordinating conjunction. Even though it's the first word in the above question, grammarians would say it connects the dependent clause, *"God is for us,"* to the independent clause, *"who can be against us."*

You may not care about the grammar, but you should care about the promise—or really the lack of promise. As written, Romans 8:31 doesn't necessarily say *"God is for us."* The conjunction "if" is describing the conditions under which something may or may not happen.

All that to say, the question lingers. *Is God for us or not?* If He is, then Romans 8:31 tells us we can live without fear. If He is not on our side, then we're in deep weeds and easy targets for Satan's evildoing.

One way to prove that God is, indeed, on our side is by looking at history. God made us, in His image no less, so that's a good sign. As the bumper sticker says, "God don't make no junk!" Also, after creating this incredible planet, He put mankind in charge. (See Genesis 1:27–28.) This also suggests we have value in His eyes.

What's more, at the moment of personal justification, God grants each new Christian at least one spiritual gift. That could be the gift of encouragement, generosity, discernment, healing, or any number of extraordinary abilities. Receiving such gifts suggests we are in His favor.

But the greatest proof that God is for us is stated clearly in the next verse:

He who did not spare his own Son,
but gave him up for us all—how will he not also,
along with him, graciously give us all things?
—Romans 8:32

That should remove any doubt. God is undeniably for us. Romans 8:32 confirms that He so loved the world that He gave His one and only Son on our behalf.

In these consecutive verses, the facts line up one after another. God sacrificed His Son for us. Which means God is for us. Which means God will allow nothing to stand against us. Which means God will graciously give us all things.

Those following this logic might see that another question has been raised: What does Paul mean when he writes *"all things"*? All things could mean He will give us everything we want. Or everything we need. Or even everything there is.

Getting "everything we want" or "everything there is" would be overwhelming and probably not a good idea. History suggests most people can't handle getting a surplus of resources. Consider the dismal fate of lottery winners, second-generation billionaires, and teenagers who get everything they want. It is better to get exactly what we need: no more, no less. Having just enough will better equip us for our God-given work.

In our new life in Christ, God has given us assignments. First Corinthians 7:17 says, *"Let each person lead the life that the Lord has assigned to him, and to which God has called him"* (ESV). If we're part of His plan, we can be confident that He will *"graciously give us all things,"* which includes everything we need to live for Him, everything we need to tell others about Him, and everything we need to successfully complete our duties on earth and make our way to our heavenly home.

GOING DEEPER:

Stick with me for one more grammar lesson. Shortly after these verses, we have several examples of rhetorical questions. This is a question proposed with dramatic effect to emphasize a point and deliver a truth that is self-evident. Examples in popular culture are "Is the sky blue?" and "Do you think money grows on trees?"

Roman chapter 8 asks three rhetorical questions with unambiguous answers:

Who will bring any charge against those whom God has chosen? It is God who justifies. (v. 33)

Who then is the one who condemns? No one. Christ Jesus who died—more than that, who was raised to life—is at the right hand of God and is also interceding for us. (v. 34)

Who shall separate us from the love of Christ? Shall trouble or hardship or persecution or famine or nakedness or danger or sword? (v. 35)

The passage ends with a bit of a battle cry knowing we are empowered by God's love and purchased by the blood of Christ. *"No, in all these things we are more than conquerors through him who loved us"* (v. 37).

Another bit of wisdom tucked into Romans 8:31–32 is the idea that God has given us the priceless gift of His Son and therefore anything else we need or ask for is a mere pittance by comparison. Refusing to meet our needs would be like giving someone a Lamborghini and refusing to fill the tank for windshield wiper fluid. A telling quotation by Martin Luther is, "One drop of Christ's blood is worth more than heaven and earth."

58

God said to Moses, "I AM WHO I AM."
—Exodus 3:14

While tending his father-in-law's flock, Moses finds himself on Mount Horeb, drawn to a bush that's on fire, but not burning. Exodus 3:4 records the first conversation between God and Moses: *"God called to him from within the bush, 'Moses, Moses!' And Moses said, 'Here I am.'"*

During the extensive conversation that follows, God gives instructions while Moses makes excuses. God expresses compassion for the Israelites enslaved in Egypt and lays out a multi-point plan for Moses to lead them to freedom. Surprisingly, even though he's talking to the Creator of the universe, Moses attempts to weasel out with statements like:

Who am I that I should go to Pharaoh and bring the Israelites out of Egypt? (Exodus 3:11)

Pardon your servant, Lord. I have never been eloquent, neither in the past nor since you have spoken to your servant. I am slow of speech and tongue. (Exodus 4:10)

Pardon your servant, Lord. Please send someone else. (Exodus 4:13)

Moses's worst whining might be Exodus 3:13: "*Suppose I go to the Israelites and say to them, 'The God of your fathers has sent me to you,' and they ask me, 'What is his name?' Then what shall I tell them?*"

Readers today might think Moses needs a trip to the woodshed, but God knew Moses's heart and had bigger plans. God's response was unequivocal and clarifying: "*I AM WHO I AM.*"

In point of fact, the question Moses asked *was* actually relevant. If he took God's message to the Israelite elders, they would need some convincing. They had been held captive in Egypt for more than four centuries, and the Egyptians had many gods with many names. There's a high probability quite a few of the Israelites had forgotten the one true God of Abraham.

With the goal of giving confidence to this inexperienced man who was being recruited to be the greatest leader of all time, God told Moses exactly what to say in the second half of that verse:

Say this to the people of Israel: "I AM has sent me to you."
—Exodus 3:14 ESV

Exodus 3:14 recognizes two major turning points for the nation of Israel. First, Moses meeting God on Mount Horeb, which set the stage for future encounters. Second, Moses taking that news back to the two million Israelites held captive and assuming his role as their leader.

Before Moses returned to Egypt, God would equip him with miraculous abilities and He even began to lay out the plan for the ten plagues to come. But the most noteworthy revelation was that Moses had been chosen by *Yahweh*, the Hebrew word for "I AM."

To further bolster his confidence and equip him to gain the ear of the elders of Israel, God gives Moses additional words to say in the next verse: *"Say to the Israelites, 'The LORD, the God of your fathers—the God of Abraham, the God of Isaac and the God of Jacob—has sent me to you.' 'This is my name forever, the name you shall call me from generation to generation.'"* (Exodus 3:15)

Something worth noting is that this extraordinary first dialogue between Yahweh and Moses through the burning bush also includes the first mention of the promised land, *"a land flowing with milk and honey"* (Exodus 3:17).

GOING DEEPER:

God's identity as the Great I AM is a precursor to many of Jesus's most profound statements in the New Testament.

I am the bread of life.	(John 6:35)
I am the light of the world.	(John 8:12)
I am the gate for the sheep.	(John 10:7)
I am the good shepherd.	(John 10:11)
I am the resurrection and the life.	(John 11:25)
I am the way and the truth and the life.	(John 14:6)
I am the true vine.	(John 15:1)

These seven statements say so much. Jesus satisfies our spiritual hunger. He delivers us from darkness. He protects us from predators and opens the gates of heaven. He rescues us when we wander. He conquered death. He connects us to the giver of life.

Through Moses, the Great I AM led the nation of Israel out of slavery, through the Red Sea, through the desert, and to the promised land. Through Jesus, the Great I AM leads all believers to freedom, through our most challenging and darkest days, and to the promise of eternal life with Himself, Yahweh.

> God chose Moses not because he was a great leader, but because he would become a great leader.
> If you're feeling ill-equipped for something God is calling you to do, go ahead and whine a little. Like Moses, feel free even to make an excuse or two. But then get over it. Whatever God has planned for you, He will empower you and equip you to get it done.

59

I have fought the good fight, I have finished the race,
I have kept the faith.
—2 Timothy 4:7

This verse occurs at a gut-wrenching moment. Paul, who has arguably done more for advancing the gospel of Christ than anyone else, is saying good-bye. Sitting in a cold prison in Rome, he's quite sure he is soon to be executed, and this verse comes from his last recorded chapter.

Paul's impact on the world is undeniable. The Bible documents his transformation from cold-blooded persecutor of Christians to dedicated missionary, inspiring leaders of the early church. His instructive and insightful letters to struggling churches and fellow missionaries anchor the New Testament.

While we don't know exactly when and how Paul died, tradition suggests he was likely beheaded by Romans under Emperor Nero. But we do know that Paul was not afraid of death. He spoke with confidence regarding the next life. *"For we know that if the earthly tent we live in is destroyed, we have a building from God, an eternal house in heaven, not built by human hands"* (2 Corinthians 5:1).

Still, Paul wanted to make sure this second letter to Timothy was completed. The book begins with joyful reflections and advice on how to press on with bold faithfulness in the face of persecution.

Even though his imprisonment was at the hands of those who were persecuting Christians, Paul is concerned that being labeled as a criminal might dampen his witness. In 2 Timothy 1:8 he writes, *"So do not be ashamed of the testimony about our Lord or of me his prisoner. Rather, join with me in suffering for the gospel, by the power of God."*

Paul's faithfulness to the end should inspire us today. Not only as an example, but also because the same crown of righteousness he will soon be awarded is waiting for all believers. This is confirmed in the next verse:

Now there is in store for me the crown of righteousness,
which the Lord, the righteous Judge, will award to me
on that day—and not only to me,
but also to all who have longed for his appearing.
—2 Timothy 4:8

The last dozen or so verses in Paul's final letter get personal and name names. He describes the location and responsibilities of people most Bible readers may not even remember such as Crescens, Tychicus, Erastus, Trophimus, Eubulus, Pudens, Linus, and Claudia, who were all real-life heroes of the early church.

The nature of email today has distanced most of us from the idea of writing long letters, licking envelopes and affixing stamps, and waiting days or weeks for a return letter. But if you've ever come across a handwritten letter from a soldier serving in the military in World War II, Korea, or Vietnam, you'll understand the sincere emotion and stream-of-conscious reflections Paul has poured into 2 Timothy. His heartfelt words provide encouragement to anyone who chooses to be part of God's army.

GOING DEEPER:

We forget sometimes that the New Testament letters—often called the epistles—were real people writing to real people with real life needs. One last verse that stands out in this letter was Paul's request for a heavy coat that he apparently left at Troas, a port on the Aegean Sea, which he visited on both his second and third missionary voyage. *"When you come, bring the cloak that I left with Carpus at Troas, and my scrolls, especially the parchments"* (2 Timothy 4:13).

Doesn't it sound like Paul was cold in prison and wanted to make sure his parchments were in order before he left this mortal coil?

Reading those words from Paul's final paragraphs inspires me to ponder my own last words. Wouldn't it be nice to be able to echo his humble declaration with sincerity and confidence? **"I have fought the good fight, I have finished the race, I have kept the faith."**

*Consider it pure joy, my brothers and sisters, whenever you
face trials of many kinds, because you know that the testing
of your faith produces perseverance.*
—James 1:2–3

God is good. As Christians, we should stake that claim and believe
it down to our toes. All good things come from God. And only
good things come from God.

Still it disturbs me when a believer chirps, "God is good" every
time something pleasant or lucky happens. They drop their phone
on the cement and it survives without a scratch. The sun comes
out just as they spread the picnic blanket. They find an unexpected
twenty-dollar bill in their blue jeans. "God is good," they say.

Those well-meaning Christians are right, of course. God is
good. But their words suggest that if the phone shattered or the
picnic got rained out or their pants pocket contained only used
Kleenex, then God might not be so good after all.

Saying "God is good" after a nice occurrence is easy and obvious. But James 1:2 is telling us to think, say, and believe God is
good after experiences that are not so nice at all. Taking it one step
further, we're supposed to go beyond finding good in our trials all
the way to considering it *"pure joy."*

James 1:3 goes on to tell us why. Trials reveal your true colors.
The testing of your faith exposes your strengths and weaknesses.

When you face a trial you will likely find out the chink in your armor, the place where you are most susceptible to Satan's tempting. When bad stuff happens, do you get angry, depressed, impatient, cynical, or abusive? Do you feel sorry for yourself, turn to drugs or alcohol, or cast blame? Or do you ask yourself, *What is God trying to teach me here?*

Truth be told, there's very little personal growth during seasons that are all sunshine and roses. It's the challenges of life that force us to dig deep, sharpen our tools, and trust God.

When our faith is tested, we will either press on with determination or not. The benefits of perseverance are spelled out in the next verse:

Let perseverance finish its work so that you may be mature and complete, not lacking anything.

—James 1:4

That's a pretty far leap and a pretty sweet deal. In just a few steps, James seems to be offering believers the ability to trade *"trials of many kinds"* for a mature life that is *"not lacking anything."* Follow the logic and that's the promise.

This passage is one of those step-by-step formulas sprinkled throughout Scripture: "If this, then this, then this, then this." Paraphrasing James 1:2–4, we might say, "Difficult challenges strengthen our faith, which brings perseverance, which leads to maturity, which results in having everything we need, culminating in pure joy."

So next time you're facing a trial of many kinds or any kind, expect joy. Then turn your full attention to applying your faith to overcoming that obstacle or challenge. That's the pathway to being a mature and complete Christian.

GOING DEEPER:

In your quest for *"pure joy"* and *"not lacking anything,"* does that mean you should go out and seek trials? Well, maybe. And you won't have to look too far.

There is a constant invisible battle to be fought with trials to overcome. That conflict is not for the faint of heart or for those who are easily duped. Ephesians 6:12 describes the battle: *"For our struggle is not against flesh and blood, but against the rulers, against the authorities, against the powers of this dark world and against the spiritual forces of evil in the heavenly realms."*

As frightening as that sounds, do not fear. Hang on to the promise of James 1:2–4, and you can face that trial with confidence and pure joy. Psalm 18:39 confirms that you are well-equipped for battle, and victory is imminent: *"You armed me with strength for battle; you humbled my adversaries before me."*

> The theme of perseverance is a good way to end this book. I'm glad you forged on to the end. I already have confidence that God used every single verse set forward in these pages. Isaiah 55:11 promises, "My word that goes out from my mouth...will not return to me empty, but will accomplish what I desire and achieve the purpose for which I sent it."

ABOUT THE AUTHOR

After a decade of penning advertising campaigns for airlines and beer, Jay Payleitner became a freelance radio producer, working for Josh McDowell, Chuck Colson, Voice of the Martyrs, Bible League International, and others. He is a popular speaker on parenting, marriage, creativity, and getting life right. Jay has authored more than twenty-five books including *52 Things Kids Need from a Dad, The Prayer of Agur, The Jesus Dare,* and *What If God Wrote Your Bucket List?* He's a longtime partner of Iron Sharpens Iron and the National Center for Fathering. Jay and his wife, Rita, live near Chicago where they raised five kids, loved on ten foster babies, and are cherishing grandparenthood.

MESSAGE FROM THE AUTHOR

If one of these chapters had a meaningful impact for you or if you happen across another instance in which a "next verse" delivers a surprise, delight, or personal challenge, please let me know.

You can track me down at jaypayleitner.com.